Mentoring into Vocation

Mentoring into Vocation

Touchstones for the Journey

Revised Edition

MARK A. FOWLER

*To Loretta —
with regard
Mark Fowler*

General Board of Higher Education and Ministry
The United Methodist Church
Nashville, Tennessee

The General Board of Higher Education and Ministry leads and serves The United Methodist Church in the recruitment, preparation, nurture, education, and support of Christian leaders—lay and clergy—for the work of making disciples of Jesus Christ for the transformation of the world. Its vision is that a new generation of Christian leaders will commit boldly to Jesus Christ and be characterized by intellectual excellence, moral integrity, spiritual courage, and holiness of heart and life.

The General Board of Higher Education and Ministry of The United Methodist Church is the church's agency for educational, institutional, and ministerial leadership. It serves as an advocate for the intellectual life of the church. The Board's mission embodies the Wesleyan tradition of commitment to the education of laypersons and ordained persons by providing access to higher education for all persons.

Scripture quotations are taken from the NEW REVISED STANDARD VERSION of the Bible. © 1989 by the Division of Christian Education of the National Council of the Churches of Christ in the U.S.A. All rights reserved.

ISBN 978-0-938162-73-5

Produced by the Office of Interpretation
Manufactured in the United States of America

CONTENTS

FOREWORD

More than twenty-five years ago, as a young pastor, I got a coffee mug that had embossed on it a frazzled-looking cartoonish character who was desperately trying to hold on to and climb a ladder. The ladder appeared to have a few broken rungs. The text coming out of the mouth of our frazzled friend read, *"I need a mentor."* The mug, along with others, always sat on a shelf in my line of sight, in several different offices that I occupied. As I recall, the mug only occasionally was used to hold a beverage. But seeing the mug on a regular basis reminded me of my need for mentoring. It also reminded me of my calling to be a mentor. And not infrequently, it reminded me of how much my life, faith, and vocation have been gifted with receiving mentoring and being a mentor.

I am sure that along the journey I could have been a more intentional and effective mentor. But of this I am also sure: I have never been short on having mentors. Not just any mentors, but great mentors. I have experienced excellent mentoring in the embrace of a loving family, outstanding congregations, patient and skillful Christian educators and youth workers, and those who have supervised my ministry. I have learned so much, even if not all I could have. I can only say, "Thank you, God, and thank you, mentors."

Reading Mark Fowler's book has not only evoked my gratitude for all I have received but also reminded me how mentoring is laced through all that the church is, does, and is called to be. He has once again contributed substantively to the church's conversation about and practice of mentoring. Reminding us that our vocation as Christians is rooted in baptism, Dr. Fowler takes us deep into the water. In a scholarly, thoughtful, and pastoral way, characteristic of who he is, Dr. Fowler takes the measure of mentoring through personal story and attention to multicultural practice, to classical definitions and Christian appropriation. In so doing he reminds us that as people of the Book, we have been called and mentored into vocation. We *are* because we *have been mentored*. Our primary vocation is to live fully into our baptism. All else flows from that.

The way in which Dr. Fowler grounds his discussion of mentoring obliterates any notions we may have that the purpose of mentorship is success according to some worldly standard. No, the end of mentoring is to fulfill our vocation as the baptized and any particular callings that may flow from that. But the purpose of mentoring is not to assist in the rise to the next rung of some ladder labeled "career." Rather, the purpose is journeying alongside the mentored to the end that each assumes the vocation of being a full-time Christian.

Mentoring into Vocation: Touchstones for the Journey will inspire and equip those who have designated mentoring roles in local churches, districts, annual conferences, and seminary communities. But true to one of its stated purposes, it will also quicken the *whole people of God*, especially local congregations and faith communities, to claim with reinvigorated intentionality their role in mentoring.

Whenever I participate in a service of baptism, I still get a bit weak in the knees when I say or hear the words of commendation. They remind me and the community both of the great privilege we have and the weighty responsibility we shoulder to join the Holy Spirit of God in making Christians. Listen to these words again.

Foreword

Brothers and sisters,
I commend to your love and care
These persons whom we this day receive . . .
Do all in your power
To increase their faith,
Confirm their hope,
And perfect them in love.
(*The United Methodist Book of Worship*, 48)

Mentoring into Vocation will help us one and all to assume this holy and essential responsibility with fresh wisdom and strength. But most of all, with love and joy.

—Bishop Gregory Vaughn Palmer
Illinois Episcopal Area, The United Methodist Church

INTRODUCTION

Why This Book at This Time?

It is a brief four years since the first edition of this book was published. The formative forces that informed the original work were born in the 1996 General Conference of The United Methodist Church. In that conference the church adopted a study of baptism, *By Water and the Spirit*, and adopted two distinct orders of ministry: the permanent deacon and the itinerant elder. These actions precipitated a renewal of focus by pastors, clergy mentors, academic advisors, and seminary site supervisors on the theological source and content of the mentoring relationship when it pertains to those sensing a "call to ministry."

As this second edition is being published, the need for a focus on the work of discerning the call of a disciple of Jesus Christ and nurturing it into a vocational path is even more acute. The United Methodist Church has extended the work of the Study of Ministry Commission in order to continue the work of clarifying the "ordering of our ministry," which will have major implications for leadership and ecclesiology. We see an increasing percentage of students who are entering our seminaries who will not enter the ordained ministry of the church, but will find other forms of leadership and service. The categories of those who serve in "pastoral roles" are caught between the pragmatic missional needs of the denomination and the ecumenical ecclesiological theology that

1

The United Methodist Church so dearly seeks to establish. This leads to the need to clarify the authority of licensed and ordained leadership as well as the role and place of sacramental theology.

All of this comes in an age when younger leaders, who are being raised up and nurtured by the church, have much less interest or trust in structures and the "orders" that accompany them. In my work in vocational formation and church leadership at Garrett-Evangelical Theological Seminary, it has become clear that students have a zeal for ministry and some form of Wesleyan connection. However, fewer and fewer are as zealous for the traditional style of "sanctuary-based" ministry and the "ordered ministry" and hierarchical connectionalism that accompanies it. The desire for connection is clear. The commitment to the machinery and authority of connectionalism as it is currently experienced is rapidly diminishing. Therefore, the need for the work of mentoring into vocation has become more intense as an imperative of the baptismal covenant of Christ's ministry in the world, let alone formation for leadership in the institutional church or the apostolic expression of ministry in evangelism and mission. A renewed commitment to nurturing the ministry claims of baptism for vocation is the wellspring of promise, renewal, and hope for the ministry of Christ in the world and the life of the church.

The work on this second edition of *Mentoring into Vocation* has been accompanied by a difficult journey through my daughter's living with Hodgkins lymphoma for the past two years. I am completing this manuscript as we observe a month's passing since her death. She was nineteen. Moriah said at the time of her diagnosis, "I believe in Christ. In the resurrection I was promised that I get life either way. So I choose to live!" I was amazed and humbled by the depth of faith that gave her the courage to live fully in those two years. Her journals and notes on biblical verses witnessed a deep and purposeful relationship to Christ through the living Word. But more to the point of this book is the importance of the role of her mentor Karen Bender and the confirmation class mentoring group that was formed at First United Methodist Church in Lancaster, Pennsylvania. The deep bond of that group was forged in a youth mission trip under Karen's leadership. Perhaps it is foundational to understand the bonds of mentoring in the common mission beyond the immediate relationship. The group met for their confirmation class, but continued to meet weekly before school for the following two years. They shared their joys and struggles and the intersection of faith with their experience and life choices. Once they graduated from high school there was a challenge in regular meetings, but the group continued and the scope of discussion broadened as the experience of life demanded more. Faith and experience informing each other was critical to them. During this period of time Moriah and I were in London, preparing for a travel class I would teach for the seminary. We found ourselves in John Wesley's bedchamber at City Road. It was the small room in which he died. Moriah read his dying words, "The best of it is, God is with us."

"Those are the words we live by in our group!" she said. "They hold us together and keep us going!" Her dimples were showing as she discovered the source of these words. The promise of baptism, embraced at confirmation, mentored and discipled for the living of these days is critical to the life of discipleship in the world, the renewal of the church, and the formation of leadership. If this book makes a small contribution to finding our way through the chaos and currents that face the church and its members in the present age, then the debt of gratitude is to the great cloud of witnesses whose lives have been dedicated to the vibrant witness of Christ and the formation of leaders that inspire this work. To Christ be the glory!

I must give particular gratitude to the work of the former Ministry Preparation Resource Team of the General Board of Higher Education and Ministry of The United Methodist Church as it worked to conceive, clarify, resource, and respond to the denomination's commitment to preparing persons for ministry in the church, especially in the area of clergy mentoring. I am grateful to have served as a charter member of that team. I am also blessed to have James Haun as a colleague at the seminary as he expands the focus on mentoring by developing training protocols for the complementary work of coaching. The need for this book has been harvested from the desire for rooting the team's work and the church's mentoring practice in the biblical, historical, and spiritual commitments of the church and a heartfelt vision and commitment to its future. The roots of calling or vocation are seen in the covenant of baptism as understood by the primitive church and renewed in the ecclesiology of the Protestant Reformers. Therefore, the focus of this work is not only for those who are seeking ordination because they have identified a "call to ministry." It is also rooted in the "priesthood of all believers" that is inherent to the baptismal calling in which persons who are part of the covenant called *church* might expect to be "mentored into vocation."

Therefore, a central focus of this book is baptism and its dynamic relationship to vocation as the calling of all Christians. The role of the mentor is manifold in biblical and ecclesial history, yet it has blossomed most abundantly in business, teaching, coaching, and other arenas in recent years. This book will seek to distinguish the role of mentoring in a Christian context.

Through the exploration of five fundamental and crucial content arenas of the mentoring relationship, I introduce formative "touchstones" for discernment, formation, action, learning, and courage to act. The touchstones emerge from biblical and formational patterns in the Christian tradition. These are Call, Covenant, Context, Credo, and Connexion. (From here on, I will use Wesley's spelling of *connection* as *connexion* so that the *x* can remind us of the intersection of our individual journeys in vocation with the body of Christ, the church.) The biblical record is marinated in these dynamics as it narrates the journey of faith as vocation is discerned, formed, and fulfilled. This project is intended to help those entering mentoring relationships to so permeate the formation and praxis of the mentee that his or her call may be fulfilled in living into and out of vocation. As Scripture is marinated in these five elements, so the mentoring relationship needs to have the same capacity as a good marinade (a parishioner of mine taught me this insight in reflecting upon the mentoring time we shared). Marinade must last long enough to permeate the very being of the participant. It must be robust enough to make a difference. It must be sustainable enough to hold up through the process and not fall apart overnight. It must be resilient enough to withstand the heat it encounters and to improve in the heat. The exploration of these five touchstones of faithful vocational formation is provided with the goal of establishing them as the permeating content of mentoring relationships.

Who Should Read This Book?

This book is designed to be a companion to mentors and those training mentors in the substance of the mentoring relationship. My enthusiasm for the work of mentoring began very early in my pastoral ministry when a member of the church responded to the call to ministry during an annual charge conference. Since that time I have mentored dozens of persons who were discerning their baptismal vocation or deepening the integration of their faith and occupational life. I have been blessed to work with local church covenant groups that sought to engage the economic and stewardship implications of the gospel in their daily work. While serving as the pastor of local churches in the Boston area, I was able to serve twelve years as a site supervisor for one or more student interns preparing for ordained ministry each year. Part of that time I was working on my doctor of ministry, which afforded me concentrated study and supervised practice in mentoring. I moved from local church ministry to the seminary setting as director of field education at Garrett-Evangelical Theological Seminary, as vice-president for vocation in ministry at Garrett-Evangelical and director of the Institute for Transformative Leaders and Communities. The vision for these roles includes working with a broad section of the church in resourcing the formative mission of preparing and sustaining leaders for the church and the world. The touchstones outlined in these chapters guide the work. In my experience, it has become clear that mentoring partnerships are holy undertakings and sacred journeys of discovery, transformation, and courageous acceptance of vocation in Christ.

Three primary audiences exist for this project. The first audience is mentors who are engaged in ministry preparation. The Candidacy Mentor and Clergy Mentor programs of The United Methodist Church form the conceptual context. However, the concepts can be applied ecumenically as they are derived from biblical and traditional Christian sources. The second audience is seminary supervisors. Within the field education programs there are persons designated to supervise a person's work at a ministry site or to be responsible for one or another function in the personal formation of a student for ministry. The content of this book is instructive for those relationships. The third audience is the baptized membership of the church. Explicit in the covenant of baptism is incorporation into the ministry of Christ and a share in Christ's royal priesthood. That calling and particular gifts and place in the work of Christ are part of the pastoral care of the baptized.

Gratitude for a "Great Cloud of Witnesses"

As I have gathered the material for this book, I have found myself remembering the people who have been mentors to me in my life. I am convinced that it is our own mentors and the relationships we form with them that will most profoundly inform the models of mentoring we adopt for ourselves.

The Letter to the Hebrews expresses this for me in a moving and poetic way. I feel bound up together with all those who have gone before and all who come after as "brothers and sisters, holy partners in a heavenly calling, [who] consider that Jesus, the apostle and high priest of our confession was faithful to the one who appointed him" (Heb. 3:1–2). This Jesus is "the reflection of God's glory and the exact imprint of God's very being" (Heb. 1:3). As I think about the privilege of being numbered with those who are holy partners in a heavenly calling and being incorporated into the ministry of Christ, I am clearly humbled by those who have given themselves to mentor me, nurture me in my faith and calling, and join with me to be mentored and pastored on their faith journey. I hope it will be evident from the pages of this book that the "great cloud of witnesses" to whom the writer of Hebrews refers are essential to my understanding of faithful discipleship and the capacity to fulfill God's call and claim on your life in vocation.

> Therefore, since we are surrounded by so great a cloud of witnesses, let us also lay aside every weight and the sin that clings so closely, and let us run with perseverance the race that is set before us, looking to Jesus the pioneer and perfecter of our faith, who for the sake of the joy that was set before him endured the cross, disregarding its shame, and has taken his seat at the right hand of the throne of God. (Heb. 12:1–2)

In assembling gratitude for my own cloud of witnesses, I start where Paul began with Timothy, "I am reminded of your sincere faith, a faith that first lived in your grandmother *Gladys* and your mother *Ruth* and now, I am sure, lives in you" (2 Tim. 1:5; italicized names added). I know that I am not the first to substitute my own mothers into Paul's epistle. My maternal grandparents were the matriarch and patriarch of a family centered in the church and formed by its faith. A son, a son-in-law, two grandchildren, along with many other family members, have become ordained or consecrated for leadership ministry in the church. All of them would readily testify to the model of faith, the dedication to the ministry of the church, and the nurturing care in faith formation both Howard and Gladys Allen took with each of us. When I came home from college and told them of my call, my grandfather led me to the chair in which he read his daily lectionary and devotion, opened his cherished testament to the Pastoral Epistles, and had me read them. He wanted me to know what was required. God in Christ was always the first mentor to whom my grandparents gave flesh, voice, and living spirit in their way of faithfully grandparenting our lives. For that, I am forever grateful.

My mother and father, the Reverend W. Robert and Ruth Fowler, and my younger sister, Martha, raised me in the ways and faith of the church and parsonage life. The passion, commitment, difficulty, and fulfillment of serving as an ordained pastor and his family were lastingly instilled by their unfailing dedication.

Many of those with whom I have shared mentoring relationships are noted and given due gratitude and reverence throughout the body of this book. I would add to their stories a note of gratitude to the Lynn Clergy Cluster, who, as a body, took it upon themselves to mentor me and provide constant covenant in the process into ministry and whose spirit of nurture lives in and empowers me still. The encouragement of my colleagues at Garrett-Evangelical Theological Seminary and the years of serving on district committees on ministry and annual conference boards of ordained ministry, along with the generous contributions of bishops, district superintendents, clergy colleagues, and laity in partner churches, have been invaluable to the development and sharpening of my understanding of the need for continually engaging in the substance of the process of preparation for ministry as well as tuning the process. With the intricacy of process and procedure, I have often wondered if we are exhausted by building and tuning the "wheels within wheels" of denomination and seminary. This work seeks to renew the embracing of the importance of the core of our shared faith as the central focus of our work.

I especially thank President Philip A. Amerson and Dean Lallene Rector for their continued support and mentoring in this project and my vocation. President Amerson has shared exemplary models of mentoring in his leadership of the seminary and his personal relationship with me. Phil's leadership heart is in the faith journey and passion that is brought to the ministry undertaken. His companionship on the journey as pastor, administrator, friend, and brother-in-Christ takes seriously, yet with great laughter, joy, and celebration, the call, covenant, and context within which ministry is done. Phil also shares a deep commitment to The United Methodist Church and its future. Along with the denominational and ecumenical church, I owe him a deep debt of gratitude. Lallene's collegiality and friendship have grown and matured in our work together on the faculty and in recent years as part of the seminary's leadership team. The intentional time we share that nurtures our mutual commitment to the mission of the seminary, the larger devotion to educating and preparing leaders for the church and the world, along with tending to matters of the heart and spirit, exemplify discipleship as mutual mentoring. These cherished colleagues are a wellspring for the living out of a vital and committed vocation in the context of a faith community.

It is with full confidence in the resurrection that Moriah continues in the "great cloud of witnesses" for all eternity. It is from a broken heart in the wake of her death, yet a grateful spirit for the witness of her life, that I dedicate this edition to Moriah's memory. I pray that her older brother, Benjamin, will be blessed with faithful mentors and worthy companions throughout his life and be comforted by the hope of our shared faith. My deepest gratitude is to my wife, Susan Joy, who pledged at our wedding to be Sabbath to me. She has also been a compassionate and wise mentor. She has given me the gift of peace, the companionship of faith, the embodiment of the fullness of the love of God, and the patience of Job and all others who have cried out, "How long?" For her willing investment in this work (both editions), her thoughtful reflections, and the postponement of many family events so that I could write, she has my deepest gratitude.

—Mark Fowler
Evanston, Illinois
March 2010

Chapter 1

ANCIENT ROOTS YIELDING CHRISTIAN FRUITS

The Reverend Earl Beane ascended the pulpit to introduce me as the newly appointed senior pastor. Earl had admitted me to the School of Theology fourteen years before. He was also a formative presence in this church. "You have to be careful whom you admit to seminary," he said. "They may become your pastor one day." A smile crossed my face as the congregation relaxed in trusting laughter to listen to the commendation of their new leader and the hope they had for the future.

I assume that Earl went on to "gild the lily" as far as my pastoral record and the wisdom of the appointment were concerned. However, my heart and mind went elsewhere. It was the word *careful* that invited me into a deeply reflective place. Earl had used it in its popular usage to convey caution and skepticism. However, mine was a more noble experience of his dealings with me beginning so many years before. *Careful* expressed itself as "full of care." It began with authentic hospitality in providing a sanctuary for discernment. As he was talking to the congregation, my mind's eye focused on his welcoming me to the admissions office as a potential student. True joy received and pervaded the spirit that was shared. He gave a distinct gift of active listening, full attention, and inquisitive interest. The presence of the holy and the nature of the divine way were shared in the gentle process of self-knowing, articulation of call, and encouragement to embrace a direction in vocation. Although we were sitting in the admissions office of the School of Theology, it was clear that getting me to choose to come to Boston University was not the major emphasis of the conversation. Earl Beane had embraced his gift and his authority to walk with me as a companion in Christ, a servant and witness of the way of God with us, a reliable "wise one" whose blessing emerges as cherished nourishment for the soul. He listened with a discerning spirit, accompanied the struggle with a vulnerable and empathetic heart, directed and challenged with encouragement, and prodded me to rise to faith in my call and in the nurture of my gifts for vocation in ministry.

Throughout my seminary career and over the interim years when I was near the School of Theology, I would stop in to see Earl. Like so many others who have passed through his office, it was clear that we are not forgotten or marginalized just because our time at the school was through and the formal relationship had ended. The commitment to "come alongside" and "journey together" has the same intention today as it did in the beginning. The years of our time together in the same local church setting that began on the day he ascended the pulpit and made that gracious introduction enriched the relationship and my respect for Earl's gifts. He gave advice only when I asked for it. Even then it was given with humility and an empowering word, reminding me that *I* was the one who had to act at this place and time as the pastor and leader of the congregation. He reminded me of the catalog of gifts and challenges that had been given to me and used in ministry over the years. Drawn from that gathering and recounting of my gifts, he helped me to frame, articulate, and claim what was entrusted to me to do.

Even to this day, when he no longer needs to be "careful" about this particular visitor's admission to the School of Theology or the future viability of my pastoring him, the opening of the door is the divine hospitality to the sanctuary of discernment. It is a place where the journey of faith is cherished, tested, searched, accounted, confessed, refined, and blessed to the fulfillment of a vocation in God. Many people come alongside each of us in our journey into discipleship and vocation. In the course of this book I will lift up accounts of many of those who have contributed to my journey and understanding of what it means to mentor someone. However, it has become clear to me in the preparation of this volume that Rev. Earl Beane has framed and fulfilled in me what I seek to describe here. I am humbled to call him My Mentor.

The Classical Mentor and the Traditional *Mani* Today

Recent years have seen a renewed interest in vocationally formative relationships across many professions that have adopted the term *mentor* to describe them. These relationships are marked by the practical need of young professionals to get a foothold in their career; for others to move to a higher level in their field; for some to change career paths; for still others to be rehabilitated and reformed when hard times, either personal or professional, befall them; and for chief executives to maintain a competitive edge aided by the voice of inspired coaching. The diversity of relational skills and training tasks applied in tutor teaching, coaching, supervising, managing, governing, apprenticing, counseling, consulting, orienting, and guiding have been sifted together and framed in the classical role of a mentor. Each field and profession has developed mentoring to meet particular ends. Teachers look to greater effectiveness in the classroom; military officers enhance the capacity for command and control to meet operational objectives; business executives seek more effective skills to fulfill the vision of the corporation through a particular array of personnel management techniques, strategic planning, and program development fitted to the situation.

One particular member of a church I served had been informally recruited by the women in her corporation to mentor new female employees so that the "glass ceiling" would not deter them in their career trajectory. Her major task was to help them find the inner courage to look through this historic boundary and reach for the highest offices of the organization. In the churches I have served, I was privileged to pastor a variety of persons who were cast in the role of formal or informal mentor. They were acutely aware of the responsibility for the individual in their charge, the needs of the greater institution, and the focus this responsibility required of them. In our pastoral conversations together, I was struck by the study, reflection, and investment they were making in their mentees.

These mentors were impressed by my interest in their work. What emerged was a need and desire that I make myself available as a mentor to these mentors. Indeed, mentors in the varied professions share seminal similarities.

The mentoring relationship is considered necessary for effective formation as a leader in the field. Even in decidedly secular contexts, the personal relationship of a mentor and mentee is portrayed as sacred and transformational. The wisdom, experience, and skill in keenly observing the life and work of the mentee are cherished gifts. The capacity to listen and reflect; to critique and reprove; to encourage and empower; and to assimilate experience, history, and theory in personally challenging, nurturing, and growth-producing ways are essential skills for mentors. The most gifted mentors are portrayed as selfless, more interested in the experience and discoveries of mentees than in their own accomplishments. Cherished mentors bring vast experience and wisdom, which they offer in humility and without hesitation for the growth, understanding, and use of the mentee. Mentors are able to embrace the future in which their mentees will lead and flourish even if the mentor will not be present to enjoy the fruits.

The original concept of a relationship designated by the term *mentoring* has been with us for 3,500 years. It is a gift from the annals of Greek mythology. The Homeric epic of Odysseus generated it. Mentor was the trusted and wise teacher of the hero's son, Telemachus. As the mythological epic unfolded, Mentor's story established the patterns of relationship that still form the fundamentals of mentoring in our current appropriation of the practice. The story of Mentor's relationship to Telemachus is filled with commendable virtue. But it is also rife with cautions that remain for us to consider as we maintain this classical term. The mentoring relationship is clearly built on guardianship, trust, care, intimacy, and other binding cords. As in any relationship when power, trust, and intimacy are factors, extraordinary care must be exercised to maintain the "rightness" of the relationship.

The epic leads us to the blessings as well as the dangers. The primary responsibility for tending it falls to the one in power, in this case the mentor. It is clear in the original tale of Mentor that the relationship could so easily be subtly corrupted from the role of being wise, guiding, and instructive to a role that replaces or obscures the virtuous, the gods, and the divine purpose. In this way, Mentor not only was wise and dedicated to effectively imparting wisdom as empowerment but also, insidiously for Telemachus, became wisdom itself. Mentor was a faithful and perceptive counselor on the journey *and* became the path of the journey itself. Mentor was a partner and guide in seeking the template of the gods in the formation of vocation *and* also became one like god to Telemachus.

On the way to the city from the airport in Cape Town, South Africa, we passed a fenced-in, neglected, open savanna. Young men were dressed in the colorful, traditional custom of their tribe. The taxi driver pointed them out and told us that they had entered the transition to adulthood. Their families gave them up to the care and instruction of the elders. Now they were to be in the wilderness for a time to build their shelters and survive on their own. This land was the traditional "wilderness" that had been neglected by authorities who did not honor this tradition. Yet, the rituals and trials persisted. During this time in the wilderness, another young man who had recently been through the same process would come to seek after their well-being. His role was to guide them through the physical challenges but, more important, to inquire about what was going on "inside" during the trials of those transitional days. These rituals and relationships are repeated throughout Africa. When the trial is completed, the young men are accorded a place among the responsible ones of the community, able to gather under the tree where the great issues of the people are decided.

This tradition is more ancient than the myths of Greece. To this day, the tradition of the extended tribal network taking responsibility for teaching, guiding, parenting, and initiating the child into his or her place and responsibility plays a large role in African identity. The elders and wise ones who pass on the tradition are respected to the level of veneration. When I visited small villages in the remote areas of KwaZulu-Natal (a province in the eastern part of South Africa), the younger members of the community eagerly fetched the mentors of the village to meet me. They were introduced with joyful pride. I got the sense that if I came to know these cherished ones, then I would know the heart of these gracious people.

I asked my venerated host how he came to be so well loved. He carefully and colorfully "beaded" the vision of the responsibility of the community to raise a child and the requirements for the elders in that process. I use the verb *beaded* advisedly, as beadwork communicates the colorful patterns of life in Zulu culture and was the occupation of many hands as this conversation unfolded. At the end of the conversation, I was blessed with the gift of a beaded "binding cord," given as a reminder of the faith that tied us together.

However, in this village many of the men had been taken to the gold mines in Johannesburg and lived in the townships under the apartheid economic scheme that destroyed traditional community and culture. My host was one of the few men left and had to assume the role that would normally be shared by many. He reminded me that he had greeted me with "What's happening?" in English. I was later to learn that the Zulu question posed by the older youth and elders to the younger members who are passing through the test of maturity is a question "of the heart": "What's happening?" It springs from the ancient traditions expressed in Swahili as *Habari gani menta.*

The Afro-centric focus of *Habari gani menta* gives us a richer context within which to explore the dynamics of the mentoring relationship. It also has as its core a more empowering focus. The relationship in Greek mythology has many of the virtues commendable to a mentoring relationship, but we have noted that Mentor never asks a question of Telemachus. His mentoring is more didactic in a way that assumes that a mentor has a clean slate upon which to write, an indistinguishable lump of clay to be formed. It is as if the mentor has it all and needs simply to "pour" it into the mentee, taking care only that it is retained.

These images are not entirely helpful for our appropriation of mentoring in the contemporary church. They lead to the false (and theologically suspicious) illusion that the mentor is the one who *does* the formation. The *Habari gani menta* role is one of a wise companion who seeks the heart with a question, "What's happening?" It is designed to open a person to his or her own experience, to discover the depth of wisdom embedded in the traditions and guidance that has been rendered, and to encourage a person to assume the responsibility of adulthood for himself or herself and in his or her own understanding. The traditional African

14

model shares the alliterative similarity of *menta* and easily stands together with Mentor as informative of how the role is appropriated in contemporary practice.

The Role of Mentor Adapted to Christian Culture

It seems prudent and wise to distinguish what Christians might mean when adopting, describing, and transforming the role of mentor as a formational concept for empowering Christian vocation. The roots are classical and traditional, but their adaptation to formation for Christian vocation must be done with some careful grafting to the rich and distinctive Christian story. Classical, traditional, and secular models should not be embraced as a wholesale and efficient replacement for the rich tradition of the church. These concepts of mentoring may frame and revive Christian practices in dynamic and fruitful ways but should not ignore the seminal blessings of the tradition. The story of faithful companionship on the journey of fulfilling the call and mission of God are not occasional offerings in the canon of the Christian tradition or the sporadic experience of the people of God. The importance, value, and substance of covenant companions in the life of the Hebraic and Christian faith traditions have been modeled since the Garden of Eden. They are the great cloud of witnesses who accompany us most closely in our work together with those who are discerning their call, vocation, and mission in Christ. If we graft the concept of mentor into our Christian tree, then let us acknowledge that the seed of the relationships we are seeking to describe was planted in Eden. The seedling was transported and transplanted by Sarah and Abraham and their descendants. A righteous branch grew from the stump of Jesse, who taught us that the seed would fall into the earth and die so that it could bear much fruit. The abundance of that fruit has been nurtured in the spiritual, missional, vocational, and faithful fellowship of the church to this day.

It has become helpful to focus our contemporary work of Christian vocational discernment and empowerment by adopting the classical term and general concept of mentoring. The term was introduced to The United Methodist Church as the protocols for nurturing new persons into consecrated and ordained ministry were developing in the 1970s and

1980s. By the time mentoring was firmly and widely established in the United Methodist lexicon for *candidacy mentors* and *clergy mentors* in 1996, it had already been a successful model of nurturing effectiveness and maturing gifts in other professions and in popular culture. Mitch Albom's *Tuesdays with Morrie* spent weeks on the bestseller list; and throngs awaited the *Star Wars* prequels as Yoda and Obi Wan Kenobi vied with Darth Vader in the struggle of the positive side of "the force" with the "dark side" in the unfolding of the mentoring of Luke Skywalker.

I hope that the intention of the church in its use of the term and concept was to use and transform the classical or even popular models in the same way Paul borrowed what was established in the classical world at the Areopagus in Athens and used it as an instrument of Christian instruction, invitation, and formation. (See Acts 17:24–28.) Here Paul reminds us how we too might appropriate the classical to the Christian.

As we consider the role of mentoring into Christian vocation, we must be very cautious that it is not co-opted for means and ends other than those embraced by an understanding of our baptismal faith, calling, and vocation. United Methodist candidacy and clergy mentors must be careful not to ultimately serve the transitory needs of the church. There are enormous pressures within the church to grow numerically or to persuade persons to embrace the "politically" or "theologically" efficient position of the day. It is a great and seductive temptation for the mentoring relationship to be used to screen for certain capacities to fulfill these ends. Mentors must be scrupulous to resist these pressures and focus, on the one hand, on the sacred role of one who is entrusted with the confidence of God and the church—the mentor—and, on the other hand, on one who seeks to respond to God's grace with the gift of his or her life—the mentee. It is a sacred task that requires exquisite attention. The role of the mentor is to be a companion for discernment and growth in discipleship toward fulfillment of a call to vocation in Christ.

It may be a coincidence, but the story of Mentor and Telemachus was reintroduced to popular culture in a "Christian" country by a distinguished leader of the church and the state in seventeenth-century France. François Fénelon was an archbishop and influential member of the court of Louis XIV. He couched his harsh critique of the monarch in a retelling of the Telemachus story. It is not so much the political intrigue that followed the publication of this very popular book that should interest our consideration of Fénelon. The intrigue is simply an entrance into reflecting on the larger ministry of Fénelon. He was unique in his time and office as he placed fundamental importance on spiritual formation for the Christian life. He was not as interested in a person's formal relationship with the church as he was in the formation of the soul to "pick up the cross" daily. By this he meant that a Christian should put aside those things that interfere with receiving the love of God in his or her heart.

Further, Fénelon renewed a popular interest in the important role of people who taught and guided persons to continually assess their gifted-ness and discern their vocation as a response to God's call. He gave credit to the director of the seminary, M. Tronson, who took care to nurture the practices of piety, the virtues of a priest, and the importance of doctrine to bring surety and guidance in Christian formation. The relationship of Tronson and Fénelon merged the gifts of a preacher, a persuasive spiritual teacher of the faith, and a person who sought the formation of another's soul in relationship with God. Tronson exhibited the qualities of mentor as a Christian companion who was a spiritual guide, an evangelist, and a teacher in the life of faith and mission.

Fénelon's ministry was being lived out during very difficult and in-tolerant days in France, when the crown revoked the Edict of Nantes. The Edict had granted the right for Protestants (Huguenots) to enjoy the rel-ative freedom of their own worship in a heavily Roman Catholic country when enmity between Catholics and Protestants was a deadly reality throughout Europe. The horrifying severity that was used by the author-ities to compel Huguenots to reject their Protestant faith and embrace the Catholic Church following the revocation is painfully remembered to this day.[1] However, even as a prelate charged to compel Protestants to conver-sion by any method, Fénelon was not as interested in the formal require-ments of compliance to the doctrines and practices of the church. His concern was more in the relationship of a person with God through the church. Protestant authors in the *Encyclopedie des Science Religioeuses* noted that he was due acknowledgment for his lack of severity and adop-tion of his methods that seem more like spiritual inquiry and teaching and seeking the "right" for another.[2]

It may seem strange to visit with François Fénelon as we consider mentoring in the contemporary church. After all, I came upon his contribution to the subject only because he had written a political broadside by reviving an ancient myth that included our subject, Mentor. In itself, that is not enough to commend him as one of our "cloud of witnesses." However, Fénelon does bring us an example of the importance of spiritual companions who help us focus on what is seminal in the formation of the Christian soul, Christian discipleship, and Christian vocation. Fénelon's pastoral leadership was characterized in his piety, preaching, evangelism, and catechesis by setting to the side the polarizing fixation on embracing a particular ecclesial formal doctrine without concern for the condition of the soul. His emphasis on grace, his spiritual direction of others in knowing their own heart, and a discipleship that seeks to know God's love for itself, not for any benefit or reward—all caused him to be appreciated and respected by formative leaders in such disparate arenas of the church as the high church movement, the Quakers, and the Methodists. John Wesley was most taken by Fénelon's piety and practice of simplicity. In his letters, Wesley commended this practice as a discipline of discipleship.[3]

Fénelon's ministry reminds us that the end of mentoring is not to make more effective leaders for the church if effectiveness begins and ends in any other measure than faithfulness to God, God's call and claim, and the offering of one's whole self in gifted service. Nor is it to advance persons in their careers or rehabilitate them in their practices. It is to receive the grace of God and respond to the call of Christ to fulfill our vocation.[4] It is to form the way in which we mentor, the focus of our mentoring, and the ends we seek together in light of the gospel claims and commitments rather than measures of readiness, success, and effectiveness that are born and adopted wholesale from other arenas of the culture.

I offer a final example from Fénelon's ministry as we refine the protocols and practices for mentoring and preparing persons for ministry. Despite the incredible pressures from the political and social demands upon his time, he reserved great attention for the clergy who served under him. They knew him not only as "father" but as "brother." He invested particular interest in those preparing at the seminary. He was thorough in his inquiry among the professors and supervisors in the practices of ministry regarding the gifts and qualifications of each candidate. He gave retreats for candidates and conferred with them during the time of ordination examinations. He would make himself available and was often accompanied on his walks by candidates seeking his care, counsel, and direction. Fénelon did not reserve this kind of personal ministry for the clergy but extended it to the poor and needy in his diocese, with whom he took time during visitations to local churches.

Fénelon offers us focus and clarity in our ministry of mentoring persons into vocation. Primarily, it is to know the love of God in our lives. It is to respond to that love in Christian vocation. It is to accompany one another in the journey as it is enriched and empowered by spiritual companionship and guidance. Finally, it is to maintain focus and intentionality by being surrounded by companions and witnesses who will help remove the distractions and to allow us to grow in the capacity to "magnify" God in our spirit and in our vocation.[5]

God's Companionship and the Work of Mentoring

As we begin to assemble the examples and witnesses to our ministry of mentoring, let us remember the story of the beginning. God is the author and example of the role of a mentor. God was the first companion. Although there are many examples in Scripture of what we now call mentoring, let us go back to the beginning in Eden. I remember still how the activity of God with Adam and Eve was formative in my own mentoring of a ministry candidate.

In the earliest biblical accounts, God is the principal who is the object of faith. God is also the One who articulates the blessing, shape, and purpose of life directly. God's first blessing to humanity is the *call to vocation* and the establishment of a relational *covenant*, "Be fruitful and multiply, and fill the earth and subdue it; and have dominion over the fish of the sea and over the birds of the air and over every living thing that moves upon the earth" (Gen. 1:28). God follows the call with an inventory of *gifts* that have been given in *covenant* to fulfill the vocational direction. "See, I have given you every plant yielding seed that is upon the face of all the earth, and every tree with seed in its fruit; you shall have them for food" (Gen. 1:29). In a whimsical reading of the Adam and Eve story from the perspective of one who has mentored many in their life's vocational journey, I find it somewhat comforting to know that in the very beginning, even after everything seems set and clear, unanticipated "issues" arise. They seem overwhelming—the end of a life claimed and cherished for the work of God. Much like Eve and Adam must have felt on that devastating evening when the sweetness of the apple soured as they hid from the presence of God.

In spite of God's call and covenant with us, we often feel rejected, then re-rooted, re-worked, and renegotiated many times as the journey progresses and the circumstances of life take unsuspected turns. It is important to remember that all of this "re-" work is a normal part of the journey, experienced by many who have traveled this way before us. But each of us experiences it differently, and we must cherish the difficult passages by faithful companioning even as God sought Adam and Eve when they felt the need to hide, withdraw, and wander fearfully to avoid the divine presence and claim upon them.

The lessons of the Edenic experience for mentoring became clear to me one fall as the pastoral intern in my care had returned from a summer away. The location of the experience seemed to lead to Eden's garden. During a youth trip to harvest and enjoy the autumnal pleasures of an apple orchard, I fell into intense conversation with the pastoral intern, a fellow chaperone and leader of the event. She disclosed some difficult circumstances in her personal and academic life that had led her to question her faithfulness, her worthiness to fulfill her calling, and the accuracy of the discernment we had done together during the prior year. It was clear that she had been mulling these over during her summertime away. In our first year of mentoring together, she had made some strong vocational commitments emerging from our conversations, coupled with positive experiences she had had in her ministry at the church. These now seemed to have been shaken. I could sense a distance in her; she seemed unwilling to engage with the youth. She seemed to show timidity and fear about what might come next. After some conversation, I encouraged her to venture away from the seeming safety of the mentoring relationship she had with me and spend time with the youth. She hesitatingly went off to be immersed in the youth group's work and give her ear and heart to those who wanted her time.

Several days later, she came to my office with the gift of an apple from the orchard. It became clear that apples and orchards had led her to pon-

20

der the story of Eden. She began a passionate witness without preface or a guiding reference for me to follow.

"Why didn't God just kill them both? That's what God promised!"

This was clearly not an academic exercise, nor a case study for me to unpack with her. I scrambled to catch up to where she was—and from the extremity of the situation, I had to move quickly.

"Instead, God took all of that time hunting around in the garden to find them."

She picked up the apple to emphasize the point. Garden. Apple. God hunting around. I couldn't remember the chapter and verse, but I caught up with Adam and Eve hiding from God after the forbidden fruit was eaten.

"Things weren't going to be as easy as they had been if they had followed the original plan! They had broken the rules; they had disappointed . . . betrayed . . . themselves *and* God—that's clear and unmistakable."

She began to work through the difficult and sometimes painful labor of bringing together the work of the seminary classroom with her experience and relationship with the God who has made a living claim on her life and gifts. For me, as her mentor and midwife, these were breathless moments.

"Original sin! It has always been about original sin. Systematics [theology] puts it all there. I like the feminists who don't want women to take the whole rap! That's all fine and important and all, but it isn't all of it! I think God got over the apple before we have!"

I was aware that she may be venturing into murky theological waters, but I was willing to follow her.

"The other day, at the orchard, I realized the apple had gotten stuck in my throat. I couldn't get it out. Thanks for listening to all of that. It was the kids. They didn't seem to see the apple. They wanted me to spend time with them and listen to them, to their lives. Secrets, shame, bravado to cover it up, wanting to forgive and move on. Looking for a word from me, a sign, a direction. They know the wrong in the world, and it makes them afraid. Their eyes seem to beg me for something else. They know the difficult choices. They know what it is to hide and be afraid and be ashamed. So do I! They want something from me."

She sat down and calmly yet earnestly led me through the process that occasioned this overflowing of herself, which clearly hadn't reached its conclusion.

"I went back and read the poetry in Genesis. You know, it turns to poetry when God announces that things will be different from now on. It bothered me as I was eating the sweet apple on Sunday, listening to the kids, that this could have caused such a problem. Maybe it would have been easier if we had all remained innocent, but we aren't. And those kids know that there is good and evil, and they don't want evil to be called good and destroy them. They want someone who knows the difference and who knows what to do. They need someone who knows their life! God cursed Adam and Eve with three things: death, work, and the pain of childbirth. And they had to leave the garden. But you know what the amazing thing is? God made them the clothes they needed to live outside the garden! Do you get it? God made them the clothes! My job is to make the kids clothes so that they can live outside the garden . . . or better, to help them put on the clothes God has made them."

She seemed exhausted now. She had claimed her vocation in a new way. She had grasped a vision. I wondered whether we could take a further step, but she would tell me if it was too much. I asked her what clothes God would make them. She looked at me rather disparagingly as if I had asked the impossible. Slowly she assembled the wardrobe.

"Clothe them in righteousness. I have to think about how that looks. I can't avoid the full armor of God, although I don't like the military image. But, thinking about it, I do like the image of protection and what Paul was trying to say. That's it for now."

I celebrated the spiritual work she had done and the affirmation of her ministry that had come through her work with the Genesis text. She corrected me and said that *God* was working with her through the Genesis text and that I would need to be sure that what she had experienced was true to God and not self-serving. We embarked on that reflection in our next time together. She finished with an abiding meditation that combined her own journey and experience with a prophetic sense of her work in the church and God's empowering gift in her vocation.

"I can't do youth group like the church is in the Garden of Eden anymore. Many of the parents of our youth are afraid, and they want their kids to be surrounded by a protective shield of innocence and they want the church to provide it. They don't want the youth group to touch the issues confronting these kids. It scares the parents. These are good kids, but they aren't innocent. They want to be good, most of them; but they aren't innocent. These kids don't live in the Garden. *I* don't live in the Garden. God had something for Adam and Eve to do even after the apple—something important—and gave them clothes and a place to do it. These kids know the supposed curses of Eden in their own experience. They are surrounded by senseless death. Their parents are working too hard to provide the affluent life they think their kids deserve. They don't want their parents to work so hard, but they can't see themselves living without all the 'stuff' that comes from that work. Even more weird is that they want to advocate for justice for the kids overseas who make their clothes, which they won't give up wearing. And the pain of childbirth, the confusion over good sex and bad sex and kids . . . we have a lot of work to do. And it's clearly the work beyond Eden. Do you think that it will be all right to emphasize that God made clothes rather than the judgment and the curse?" (Gen. 3:8–22).

I observed that she had already made that emphasis. Her appropriation of the story was not to twist it to her own use. She was reading the story out of her own experience. And she was allowing Scripture to read her and shape her understanding of what had happened in her own life. This vital hermeneutic was transforming and empowering for her. It would also empower the way in which the church was led and empowered in mission.

As God had companioned and mentored in the opening of Genesis, and Adam and Eve's experience is added to the "cloud of witnesses" that witnesses to our own mentoring partnerships, so it is important for anyone who enters into Christian mentoring to read Scripture in a new way. Briefly survey with me the formative stories.

As Genesis unfolds, the direct voice of God's call to vocation and covenant is sustained with Abraham and Sarah and their descendants. Under the monarchy, the prophet receives an important role that fulfills crucial functions of mentoring the leader into a vocation that is part of the covenant with God. Nathan and David provide us with a formative model of the prophetic mentor working with someone who is in a leadership position. So does the story of Elijah and Elisha. Ruth and Naomi have been cherished as a poetic expression of faith formation and faithfulness. The leadership of Queen Esther and her relationship to Mordecai has emerged in religious and secular studies as a good model for coaching and encouragement.

Luke's Gospel begins with the visitation of Mary to Elizabeth and exposes the tender, vulnerable kind of relationship that I choose in chapter 2 to help focus our consideration of the nature of mentoring in a Christian context and spirit. Paul and Barnabas; Priscilla, Paul, and the early church; the disciples as a mentoring community—all are instructive in formulating an understanding of mentors in our common canon. From our Christian confession, Jesus is the incarnate one whose way with us embodies the fundamental and seminal understanding of how we are to be with one another.

Christian mentoring finds its substance in living out the vocation of the risen Christ, into which all are baptized and have gifts for fulfillment. Christian mentoring occurs in an acknowledged faith, trusting in the counsel and wisdom of the Holy Spirit. In this way, the mentor is not the path or the chief counsel, nor the greatest wisdom or the ultimate truth. The mentoring relationship finds its purpose and fulfillment by walking and growing in faith *together*. It is an active faith, focused on discerning the decisions, direction, and commitments to be made that are the fruit of living out of our baptismal covenant. In this light, a Christian mentor is a person who expresses holy hospitality in a sanctuary of discernment and faithful commitment.

I believe that the Methodist tradition yields an important model for mentoring in the role of the early class leader and the expectations of the class meeting. These early Methodist practices have been renewed in Covenant Discipleship programs. However, my research and experience have shown that the class leader, in the context of the class meeting in the early Methodist movement, was most effective in mentoring the focus on baptismal vocation. A reexamination of the vocational aspects of these institutions is instructive to the work of mentoring.

General Conference 1996: A Watershed for United Methodist Ministry

The United Methodist General Conference of 1996 was a watershed event in renewing and reforming our understanding of Christian initiation, identity, and ministry. In addition to establishing the order of deacons and the order of elders as a new formulation of clergy leadership for the church and the mentoring programs that accompanied them, the conference also received and embraced a study document on the sacrament of baptism. A central theme in the baptismal document is the recovery of ongoing discipleship and vocation central to understanding Christian baptism. When taken together with the mentoring relationship of the preparation of clergy, it is crucial to grasp that mentoring into vocation is an imperative pastoral task inherent in the baptismal covenant. Pastoring, companioning, discerning, and mentoring the baptized to realize their calling and fulfill it in vocation is not a discrete opportunity for those called to traditional "holy" or "clerical" orders. Rather, it is essential to shepherding the whole people of God. This focus on vocation is an ongoing gift of the Reformation's vision of the church as the priesthood of all believers. It was also a focus in the structures of early Methodism. The class meeting under the vital leadership of the class leader were *collegia pietatis* (little colleges of piety) intended to form the spiritual character of a Methodist. A key focus of the class meeting was ongoing vocational discernment, formation, and empowerment as an expression of a life in Christ. In reading the accounts of the process, it is clear that the spiritual enterprise was undergirded by a conviction that work in the world was a matter divinely graced. However, in order for that grace to be effectively realized and grow in a person's life experience, the class leader and members had a critical role of mentoring, shepherding, and providing an arena for spiritual and temporal accountability.

The editor of *By Water and the Spirit: A United Methodist Understanding of Baptism*, John O. Gooch, introduced the document that was used in preparation for the 1996 General Conference with a reflection on his own growth in understanding of the central and comprehensive importance of the sacrament for the church.

> Little did I know that it was to change my whole life, cause me to rethink my faith and my theology, and lead me to a closer relationship with Christ and the church. . . . I *now* see baptism as *central* to the life of the church and the way the church nurtures its members. I believe that "living out of baptism" is a call to both personal and social holiness, and to helping nurture the lives and faith of children (of all ages) in the faith. May your study of baptism help lead you to new insights, to new faith, to a new adventure as a part of God's people.[6]

25

This captures John Wesley's conviction that baptism is the initiating part of a lifelong process of working out the salvation that has come by faith in Christ.[7] For Wesley, it begins in prevenient grace, offered freely to all. Baptism is a sacramental affirmation and response to that grace, evidenced in the fruit it bears. The United Methodist candidacy process toward ordained ministry adopts the Wesleyan focus as its pattern for the mentoring partnership. Each section of the journey is divided into consideration of *gifts, grace*, and *fruit*. The discipline is a Methodist understanding of living out one's salvation, signified in baptism, in discipleship and vocation.

The renewed emphasis on the centrality of baptism to Christian identity and the ongoing call to discipleship in the world undergird pastoral work in vocational discernment and mentoring partnerships with those who seek to discern their calling and the vocation growing out of it. "Baptism is the ritual symbol through which God claims us individually and corporatively for the ministry of all Christians. This ministry is the activity of giving our whole lives in discipleship to Christ based on an active, living relationship with God through the Holy Spirit."[8]

Baptism establishes the binding relationship of God to a Christian in the body of the church, but it articulates an imperative for engagement in the world as the believer's baptismal vocation.

> All Christian ministry is based on the awareness that one has been *called* to a new relationship not only with God, but also with the world. Christians are to embody the gospel and the Church in the world, and declare the wonderful deeds of him who called us out of darkness into light (1 Peter 2:9). We exercise our *vocation* as Christians by witnessing to Christ in our daily life and labor, as a ministry of reconciliation and peacemaking in the world. This is the universal priesthood of all believers.[9]

Baptism is incorporation into the vocation of God and the body of Christ. A person is divinely called through baptism to become part of God's acts of salvation in the world. The vocation to which God calls us is a divine means to right the fallenness of creation and community. To become part of the divine vocation through baptism and to accept the need to discern that vocation through responding to God's grace is to move toward fulfilling the vision of *shalom* and the reign of God expressed in the witness of Scripture and the promise of Christ. God's purposes in personal and communal life and in life in the world are inherent in a faithful response in vocation to the divine call and claim and to the gift-edness of our lives. Vocation, in this sense, gives a central purpose for life that is beyond the self, beyond the community, and beyond the confines of the world. Yet it invests each of these spheres with transcendent purpose and meaning.

For the church to continue to renew the fullness of the place and proclamation of baptism is to renew its promise and empowerment for participation in the divine vocation. Vocation gives meaning and significance to all of life—transcending the temporal and temporarily utilitarian and embracing the eternal meaning in God's initiative, claim, and action. Scripturally, personal vocation is part of corporate vocation, which is part of divine vocation.

The emphasis on Christian vocation in the baptismal study, coupled with the establishment of mentoring as a crucial role in the preparation for ministry, also renews the importance of the pastoral care and the emphases that were empowered in the Methodist experience by the class meeting and the class leader. The dramatic impact on the lives of Methodists and the way in which they directly affected the world through their occupations are broadly celebrated in history. Baptism's renewal and reclaiming of a Christian's occupation as intentionally understood in terms of vocation reforms and renews the secular understanding of work. It also can rehabilitate the approach to ordained ministry, seeing it as a vocation rather than primarily as a profession. In common usage, occupation and profession are often defined with reference to various skills and categories of work.

"Defining vocation as occupation allows us to restrict it largely to self-serving actions. . . . Seeing vocation as the situation in history and society in which we find ourselves enlarges it almost beyond our strength. But responding to such a calling will surely allow God to sanctify and empty us so that Christ will be all in all."[10] Grasping the vision that our work or occupation may be part of the vocation of God shapes and refines our daily investment beyond toil or self-centered achievement. It redeems the time with divine intention, shapes and forms the way in which we dispense our energy as godly commission, and empowers advocacy in the workplace in light of God's justice and intention for human endeavor.

According to Philippians 2:12, a person's vocation is determined inwardly at the point where God's willing and working are united with a person's will and work. Vocation includes the discerning of personal gifts and graces, given by God, for vocational participation in the world.[11] God has given the vocational possibility to everyone (see Paul's arguments about including the Gentiles in mission, derived from an understanding of the oneness of humanity, as from the foundation of the world). Therefore, it is possible for a person to discern his or her gifts for vocation. It is crucial to the task of the church—especially through its pastors, leaders, and those called to the specific role of mentor—to renew a culture of the call and proclaim God's yearning to include everyone in the divine vocation. We must establish an environment within the Christian community for the intimate and critical work of discerning call, grace, gifts, and vocation.

Like the Hebrews in the Exodus, when leaving a culture whose occupations were determined by the powers and principalities and moving to a place where vocation is lived as a faithful response to God, teachers and mentors help translate God's call and covenant into practical guidelines for living out our vocation. Jesus renewed this in the discipling of the apostles in the context of the mentoring and learning ecology of those years they spent together. The early church attended similar education and mentoring experiences as a hallmark of the earliest *ekklesia*. Martin Luther's reformation of the church made the Bible available in a language that folks could read and understand. It was accompanied by education and mentoring "table talk." The Methodist establishment of the Sunday school and formidable institutions of education were intended to complement the baptismal work of the class meeting with the guidance of the class leader as a most worthy preparation for ongoing response to God's overwhelming grace and bestowing of gifts. The mentoring partnerships established for ministry preparation are a focused process that begs to be renewed as part of the ongoing pastoral work inherent in the baptismal covenant of vocation, bestowed as an inheritance to all who receive the sacrament and, beyond, as a sign to the whole world of the great vocation of God in which there is a share for us all. I will rejoin the discussion of baptismal vocation in chapter 3.

Mentoring as Part of the Renewal of the Covenant of Ministry and the Church[12]

As the story of the United Methodist tradition is told, 1996 will stand as a marking point for the renewal of the covenant of ministry in the denomination. Deacons and elders became members of distinctive orders. In this reordering of ministry the importance and structure of the probationary—now provisional—process received particular focus with the introduction of clergy mentoring. Other components were to be developed and coordinated as a fourfold approach to shepherd a commissioned minister through the probationary years: clergy mentoring, covenant groups, continuing education, and supervision.

Anticipating the sweeping changes of the 1996 General Conference, the General Board of Higher Education and Ministry established a team that would work with the legislative changes and attempt to conceptualize and envision practical strategies and training protocols for annual conferences. The former Ministry Preparation Resource Team provided quadrennial training events for representatives of boards of ordained ministry and has sent teams of resource persons to train mentors, boards of ordained ministry, and cabinets in annual conferences throughout the United Methodist connexion. In the experience of this process, the reality of the reform and renewal of ministry became increasingly clear.

Members of the team have likened it to the reformation and renewal of covenant that came to the people of Israel during the reign of Josiah. The reforms under Josiah envisioned reestablishing leadership in the model of David, a cherished memory for the people. Josiah was intent on focusing the treasure of the people in renewing temple worship. The high priest Hilkiah found a copy of the Book of the Law, the foundational covenant between God and God's people, in a box of rubbish to be removed from the temple during reconstruction. Some scholars believe that the content of the scroll was the earliest form of Deuteronomy. Reading and remembering the covenant law brought Josiah to the conclusion that doom was in store for Israel. In consultation with the prophetess Huldah, Josiah's fears were affirmed. However, she gave Josiah a word of assurance that grew out of Yahweh's acceptance of the king's acts of humility, penitence, and renewal. "You shall be gathered to your grave in peace; your eyes shall not see all the disaster that I will bring on this place" (2 Kings 22:20*b*).

The worship, priestly rituals, liturgical practice, and teaching of the covenant were renewed and laid down in the Deuteronomic revision. In the retelling of the Exodus story, the writers of Deuteronomy focus the renewal as occurring at the breathless moment when the Hebrew people are poised on the plains of Moab ready to enter the Promised Land. To this day, the central affirmation of the Deuteronomic renewal, the Shema (Deut. 6:4–9), focuses the covenant of the Jewish people with God.

Centuries later, Jesus used the Shema to summarize two main principles of the commandments, placing himself solidly in his faith tradition: "Hear, O Israel: the Lord our God, the Lord is one; you shall love the Lord your God with all your heart, and with all your soul, and with all your mind, and with all your strength" (Mark 12:29–30). In these familiar words, Jesus reconfirmed that living within the covenant community means being called to love God with all one's being, every aspect of personhood. This is an especially important message for Christians living in a culture that encourages compartmentalization, leading to epidemic dissociation.

Dissociation means creating false barriers between aspects of life— emotional, intellectual, structural, ethical, even doctrinal—which enable us to rationalize the acceptability of actions inconsistent with who we claim to be. It also enables dissociation between a religious affirmation of faith and action in one's occupation or personal life. The Shema, to the contrary, is a principle of total engagement with God, declaring that the fullness of faith is found by seeking to give ourselves (*agape* love) to God with complete integrity, thereby fully discovering God's self-giving love for us as well as a way of life in supportive, caring community with our neighbors. The covenant is relational and holistic in its nature.

Jesus is the formative model for covenant ministry. The call of the disciples is the genesis of our understanding of renewal. Jesus was the formative mentor and rabbi for the apostles. Yet, we remember that when he sent them out, they went two-by-two—companions and mentors on the journey to call and disciple the people of God. This model of mentoring was perpetuated in the early church. Also, early Methodist circuit riders went with the supervision of the bishop and the connexion of ministry to mentor and empower them. These were evangelists of the grace and love of God. John Wesley's sermons overflow with Jesus' revision of the Shema and other discourses on the covenant of love between God and God's people in Christ Jesus.

The directive of the rabbis for praying the Shema may be instructive for the establishment of the disciplines of discernment of call and a covenantal response in vocation. I commend them to church leaders, pastors, mentors, boards of ordained ministry, and any others who walk the journey together in response to God's call and claim. While saying the opening phrase, the heart of the covenant, "Hear, O Israel, the LORD our God, the LORD is One," each person is to cover the eyes with his or her hands. This is intended to remind the one who prays that this formative expression of the covenant deserves undivided attention. Just so, the covenant of ministry at the heart of this process deserves the undivided attention of the commissioned minister, the mentors and partners in the process, the boards of ordained ministry, the cabinets and churches. The process and its disciplines were born in hope for renewal and transformation. The role of the mentor is to keep focused on the essential touchstones of Christian vocational formation (call, covenant, context, credo, and connexion) and be watchful that the institutional process or corrupting concerns do not distract from the fulfillment of the baptismal promise of a portion of God's vocation in the world.

The 2008 General Conference passed legislation that changed the language of the period between commissioning and ordination from "probationary" to "provisional." The term *probation* was the successor to language of "on trial." Clearly we have moved away from judicial language. But, what do we mean by provisional?

I am a native of New England. Great ships have come to port for centuries precisely for the purpose of being provisioned for the next journey. The obligation of the church is clear during this period if we adopt the language in the spirit of provisioning a ship. This is especially poignant given the image of the church as a ship that is within ecclesiastical iconography. The challenge of mentoring is clearly framed as one who guides the provisioning period, not one who prepares for the mentee to be released from probation. It also provides for understanding that "being provisioned" extends beyond ordination and is not exclusive to the clergy. Provisioning is a model for what is needed to sustain the covenant of baptismal discipleship and clerical leadership in and through the church.

Touchstones for the Journey

The discernment of God's call, the realistic assessment of gifts and their use in particular contexts, and faithful attention to nurturing Christian vocation is difficult work. If there is any clear or certain answer or path for the journey, it can be understood only in terms of faith and trust in God's mercy. However, five elements seem to recur in Scripture, historical models, and my personal experience of clergy mentoring, as well as in my vocational discernment work with laity and class meetings focused on vocation. These form essential *touchstones* to which the relationship returns again and again.

Touchstones are reference points against which future experiences can be tested and understood. They are usually excellent qualities or examples that test the genuineness or excellence of other experiences. These could be personal experiences or could be gathered from similar experiences in Scripture or Christian tradition. The term comes from the use of a hard stone, such as jasper or basalt, to test the quality of gold or silver.[13]

In what follows, I use *touchstone* to identify five aspects of the mentoring journey—call, covenant, context, credo, and connexion. These touchstones form empowering disciplines to embrace the vitality of joining the vocation of God in the world. They emerge as a capacity for commitment and faithful assurance in the use of gifts in particular contexts and encourage a holy boldness to claim and announce a credo, "Here I stand; I can do no other!" These touchstones bind us to accountability within the connexion of the church and others who are called into the ecumenical vocation of God. As a mentor travels with a mentee in discernment and maturation in his or her vocation, they will continue to gather the "cloud of witnesses" who will serve as guides and examples of genuineness and excellence and who can help frame, shape, and test the mentee's experience of call, covenant, context, credo, and connexion.

32

Call

The journey to the mentoring relationship and living out one's vocation in relationship to the call are central to the partnership. As part of the mentoring relationship, it is an ongoing challenge to discern and articulate the call. However, this is not a once-and-for-all exercise. Continuing renewal, re-visioning, and articulation of the call, refined by ministry experience and connected to the divine source, empower a vital life of ministry. God's claim and the community's response are central to reflecting on the constant need to articulate one's vocation afresh as it empowers ministry.

Covenant

A personal sense of calling and vocation is gathered up in the covenants that God has made with the community. This aspect of mentoring is both personal and communal. It centers on the way in which the scriptural covenants and the covenants of the tradition and the denomination, along with the personal sense of covenant, come together in the living church and in one's family, one's friends, and one's life in the world. Reality testing, expectations, responsibility, and conflicting priorities must be worked through as this touchstone is brought to bear. Integrity in faith and life is a focal point. Realized hope and eschatology are areas to reflect upon.

Context

As the journey in vocation—or, specifically, ministry preparation—unfolds, it becomes more and more necessary to understand one's calling and one's covenants within the immediate context in which one lives. In some ways, this is dealing with "Pentecostal fire" in that the context refines the call and covenants in particular ways. The key is to help in the process of the refiner's fire but without allowing the call or the covenant faith to be consumed. This is a time when the safety of the mentoring relationship is crucial; yet this time also requires the courage of the mentor and the encouragement needed to engage the context with one's whole self-in-ministry.

Credo

It is an important skill to locate the journey of the people of God whom we serve within the biblical, traditional, and historical narrative of the church. This stimulates dynamic and faith-empowered leadership. It is out of an understanding of the narrative that we make theological claims and stimulate imagination. With the resources of a theological education and theological imagination and systems available, the mentoring team has the ability to engage their own theological reflection in reaction to what is being experienced in context. This aspect of the mentoring relationship gives a person in ministry the courage to lead through a confident faith in what God is doing here and now. Exercising one's capacity for theological reflection and understanding in a trusted and committed relationship is vital to developing a faithful ministry of leadership.

Connexion

The vocation we claim is not our own but is understood within the larger calling and purpose of the body of Christ, the community of believers. The relationship of mentoring takes place within a larger context of responsibility to the members of a particular clergy order in the church. Although there are various levels of confidentiality, this relationship is not "secret" or "personal" but has the confidence of the entire body to nurture and mature the calling and the covenants participants have made. Further, it has the confidence of the body to develop the skills and wisdom of contextualization and the acuity, faith, and courage of standing upon and leading from the credo that emerges.

* * *

The renewal of attention to faithful companionship in the discernment and development of Christian baptismal vocation is filled with dedicated hope for the future. The role of the mentor is crucial to the preparation of clergy for ministry and is built into the structures of The United Methodist Church. However, the implications are broader and more inclusive. The mentoring model the church has embraced is not reserved for the preparation of the clergy. It has profound implications for the way

34

in which Christian leaders continue to refine their vocational understanding, the use of their gifts, and the divine claim and partnership with them in leading the body of Christ. More broadly, the ministry of mentoring into vocation is for the whole congregation of the baptized and envisions embracing the entirety of the children of God.

Notes

1. The difficult narratives from those days were shared with me in hallowed and reverent stories of the suffering endured by their descendants who, although members of a United Methodist church, were Huguenots in their identity and living ancestry. For the Huguenots to acknowledge Fénelon in even the slightest sympathetic term is testimony to his unique character during those times.

2. A brief overview of the contribution of François Fénelon can be found in *The Westminster Dictionary of Christian Spirituality* (Philadelphia: Westminster, 1983). More extensive reading is available in the *Catholic Encyclopedia* and a variety of books and resources cited by them.

3. John Wesley, *Wesley's Works* (Grand Rapids: Baker, 1979), vol. 12: 287, 329, 450; and vol. 13: 24, 28. Although Wesley seemed to include Fénelon as one who had admirable piety and commendable spiritual disciplines, he was not fully convinced that Fénelon had exhibited the fruits of his own convictions, "We [the Methodists] have all the gold that is in them [Fénelon's books], without the dross."

4. This is the outcome of the adoption of Fénelon. There is some condemnation of the formulation of Fénelon's theological and spiritual approach to the extent that it is seen as part of the movement known as Quietism. However, we cannot dismiss the focus on the gracious gift of God's love. It is the formative message of the Wesleys and the Methodist movement.

5. See Luke 1:46–55. The Magnificat frames my approach in Chapter 2, "Mentoring Into . . ."

6. Dwight Vogel, *By Water and the Spirit: A United Methodist Understanding of Baptism* (Nashville: Cokesbury, 1992), 1 (emphasis added).

7. Wesley's *ordo salutis* can be found in many of his works. However, there is a good explication in "The Principles of a Methodist" and "The Principles of a Methodist Farther Explained," found in *The Works of John Wesley: The Methodist Societies; History, Nature and Design* (Nashville: Abingdon, 1989).

Good reformed Protestant that he was, Wesley was constantly defending his conviction that justification by faith alone was sufficient for salvation. However, he would not have thrown the Book of James out of the New Testament. Wesley had deep concern about the fruits of one's salvation. These fruits are a critical aspect of Wesley's historic questions for examiners, which are still used in the candidacy process today. These questions are now the responsibility of the staff/pastor-parish relations committee to raise with a candidate for ministry. This citation and the consideration of a candidate's fruit are part of the threefold theme of *grace, gifts,* and *fruit* in the candidacy process for ordained ministry. See *Fulfilling God's Call: Guidelines for Candidacy* (Nashville: General Board of Higher Education and Ministry, 2009).

8. Vogel, *By Water and the Spirit,* 48.

9. Ibid. (emphasis added).

10. Marc Kolden, "Luther on Vocation," *Word and World: Theology for Christian Ministry* 3/4 (Fall 1983): 390.

11. Paul S. Minear, *To Die and to Live: Christ's Resurrection and Christian Vocation* (New York: Seabury, 1977), 40*ff.*

12. This section has been adapted from *Readiness to Effectiveness: Preparation for Professional Ministry in The United Methodist Church* (Nashville: General Board of Higher Education and Ministry, 2006). The writing of this work was a joint effort between the Reverend James Haun and me. This section bridges directly to the vision of the former Ministry Preparation Resource Team in the overall impetus and ethos of ministry preparation in The United Methodist Church. Mentoring is a major aspect of the program.

13. *The American Heritage Dictionary of the English Language,* 4th Edition (New York: Houghton Mifflin Company, 2000).

Chapter 2

MENTORING INTO . . .

The yearly discipline of the liturgical calendar reminds us that the beginning of the cycle is set aside for preparation, waiting, and patience. In the Christian spiritual journey, the new year does not begin with the kind of celebration that marks the secular traditions. This discipline should frame the way we view our response to God's call and claim on us. The response is not the immediate affirmation of ordination or finding immediate fulfillment in a new approach to occupation. Rather, the response begins like Advent. Advent is a time when we are called to personal reflection and attentiveness to the activity of God, awake to the coming of Christ. We look back to Nazareth and Bethlehem to prepare for the birth of Jesus and forward to the culmination in the coming fullness of Christ's reign. The hymn "Wake, Awake, for Night Is Flying" gives a vivid sense of our preparation for Christ's coming.

> Wake, awake, for night is flying;
> the watchmen on the heights are crying:
> Awake, Jerusalem, at last!
> Midnight hears the welcome voices
> and at the thrilling cry rejoices;
> come forth, ye virgins, night is past;
> The Bridegroom comes, awake;

your lamps with gladness take:
Alleluia! And for his marriage feast prepare,
for ye must go and meet him there.

Zion hears the watchmen singing,
and all her heart with joy is springing;
she wakes, she rises from her gloom;
for her Lord comes down all glorious,
the strong in grace, in truth victorious.
Her Star is risen; her Light is come.
Ah come, thou blessed One,
God's own beloved Son:
Alleluia! We follow till the halls we see
where thou hast bid us sup with thee.[1]

When I was six or seven, my grandmother sat me down in the quiet of a late Sunday afternoon. It was during the magical time between Thanksgiving and Christmas. The house was decorated, and the tree had been put up with my grandfather's meticulous care. My childish excitement and focus on those presents under the tree, the laughter at the family meal, and the wonder of it all had probably gotten the best of me that day; and I found myself sitting alone to quiet down with my grandmother. Grandma and I probably had our hands busy sorting through Christmas cards to hang by the fireplace. From memory, in a warm and comforting voice, she began the Christmas story. "In the days of King Herod of Judea, there was a priest named Zechariah, who belonged to the priestly order of Abijah. His wife was a descendant of Aaron, and her name was Elizabeth" (Luke 1:5).

Grandma warmed when she reached the section about the visitation of Mary to Elizabeth. I clearly remember her taking a handkerchief from under her watchstrap to dab at a tear when the kinswomen (at the time, I wasn't sure what that meant, but it made Grandma cry) saw each other. I had stopped my sorting and scooted closer. I said the words with her, "They went to the city of David called Bethlehem" and Jesus was born. Grandma ended, "'When they saw this, they made known what had been told them about this child; and all who heard it were amazed at what the shepherds told them'" (Luke 2:17–18).

Grandma asked me to get her Bible and find where we had stopped. "Now comes my favorite verse in the Bible." She wanted me to read it to her. "'But Mary treasured all these words and pondered them in her heart'" (Luke 2:19).

Mary treasured all of these words and pondered them in her heart.

Elizabeth as Formative Forerunner in Christian Mentoring

That one afternoon, so long ago, impressed upon me the importance of pondering and reflection in the Christian life. I also carry with me the feelings of that day, which shape my reading of the Elizabeth story. Grandma's living room was a place of absolute safety, a sanctuary where I was wanted and where I was supposed to be. Grandma gave me her undivided attention; except, I was aware that she was focused on telling me a story that flowed from deep within her and required a particular attention of its own. But it was being told for *me,* not for her. At the time, I wasn't sure why, but the events of that afternoon have clearly reached far beyond themselves; and now, in sharing them with you, they have reached even beyond me. My grandparents modeled for me the virtues Elizabeth had shown Mary in the story my grandmother had taken the time to commit to memory—not only by memorizing the words but also by making the story her own in its telling.

In forming a distinctively Christian practice of mentoring, it is important to begin where God and Christ began—by gathering a community of relations and witnesses. For me, Elizabeth is the first model of Christian mentoring we encounter in the Jesus story. There is much to learn from her and the way in which she related and responded to her kinswoman, Mary (her mentee in this context).

Mentoring into vocation relationships generally begin after some incident that disturbs the normal course of one's life. There are a variety of ways in which people experience what the tradition has come to term "call." But whether it is a clear "message from God," or "the voice of an angel," or a "disturbing feeling I couldn't resist," a vocational mentor in the Christian context is engaged in the wake of a disturbing experience of call. Mary's words in response to Gabriel's call are not uncommon. She was "perplexed." She wondered, "How can this be?" Gabriel's response indicates that she was afraid and anxious about what had come to her.

For many Christians, the announcement of the coming of Christ is an indescribable moment of joy and hope. However, like many who are called to divine vocation and to find themselves as part of the mission of God, this is a time of dislocation, confusion, and wonderment. Like Mary, many who have received a call from God find themselves distanced from their normal relationships. Recall that Mary was spared death and was dealt with "justly" by Joseph, who had decided to divorce her quietly, because he was a "righteous man." She was shamed in Nazareth. The plans and hopes for her life were dramatically changed. Nothing is the same; yet Mary accepts God's commission, "Here am I . . . let it be with me according to your word" (Luke 1:38). So it is not surprising that she "set out and went with haste to a Judean town in the hill country, where she entered the house of Zechariah and greeted Elizabeth" (vv. 39–40).

This is the moment when most mentoring relationships begin. It is a time when God's call has been received with all of the associated feelings and experiences—and a certain, often frightened and perplexed, commitment has been made. Today, for many, the lingering doubt, "How can this be?" remains. The United Methodist Church, in its wisdom, has understood the importance of a place like the house of Zechariah for someone to go to sort out, discern, and examine his or her call before revealing it to the community. The candidacy process has internalized the need for Zechariah's house, a safe place and a *sanctuary* of discernment to be provided very early in the vocational response to call. "Mentoring occurs within a relationship where the mentor takes responsibility for creating a safe place for reflection and growth."[2]

Those who seek to set up mentoring programs in their annual conferences, seminaries, or churches have often asked me to define *safe place*. It is clear to me that a safe space for mentoring begins with the understanding of a place of retreat and sanctuary. From the Garden of Eden to Zechariah's house to a space apart where the disciples met with Jesus, it is important to begin with a sacred and safe space. Earl Beane's office, my grandmother's living room, the chancel of the chapel, a walk by the lake—all are places set apart as sanctuaries of discernment where the incubation of God's call can be revealed, nourished, nurtured, and encouraged to grow.

When Mary entered her kinswoman's house, Elizabeth responded to her greeting in an amazing way. The child in her womb quickened. She felt life move in her. It is an extraordinary *hospitality.* The quality of hospitality shown to Mary opens a way in which we can enter Christian mentoring. Of course, most mentoring relationships do not involve the physical reality of two gestating children. However, the reality of the call and claim of God are very much a present reality in the mentee and in the mentor to whom he or she comes. The quickening within Mary was mirrored by the quickening within Elizabeth. The life that is renewed and reformed by the grace, call, claim, and spirit within the mentor and mentee becomes the unifying element of the relationship. Much like Elizabeth, a mentor is generally more advanced in years and/or wisdom than the mentee. Like Elizabeth, with her life linked so intimately with the formal religious structures of Israel through a priestly family, a mentor should be chosen on the basis of his or her broad knowledge of the traditions of the church, its theology and doctrine, its polity, its practices, its politics, and its community. However, the key relational element that joins mentors and mentees in Christian vocational discernment and empowerment is the living call of God and the stirring of spiritual grace within that "will not let me go!"

It is imperative that this kind of hospitality be available to those who join a mentee on the journey. The danger for The United Methodist Church in establishing mentoring as a part of the entry process into ministry is that sanctuary and hospitality as fundamental aspects of the mentoring process could be replaced by an understanding of mentoring as dealing with practicalities and peripherals. Thus these aspects are equated with hoops to jump through, a screening process, a formal step of introduction where orientation to expectations takes place, an assessment tool, or a relationship of which one is skeptical. Perhaps the shift from the juridical language of "probation" to an invitation to be "provisional" during the period from commissioning to ordination will frame the time as the practices of the "home of Zechariah" in the presence of an Elizabeth-like mentor.

Remember that Elizabeth echoed Gabriel's greeting, "Greetings, favored one! The Lord is with you" (Luke 1:28) with "Blessed are you among women, and blessed is the fruit of your womb" (v. 42). The expression of hospitality in the context of Christian mentoring is to acknowledge, to be humbled and blessed, and to stand in awe of what God has already done in the life of the one who has come to be mentored.

It is to acknowledge that the reason for the time together is to begin to discern what amazing things God's grace has done in the life of a cherished one who has yielded to the call and claim made upon his or her life. Greet the mentee: "Greetings, favored one! Blessed are you and blessed will be the fruit of God's grace working within you and through you."

As a man approaching this story, I needed a long time to understand what women who have been through pregnancy already know. When the news came that our first child was to be born, I ran to the calendar, counted out nine months, and marked the due date. I then set about a plan to prepare for this wondrous event—until I realized, in no uncertain terms, that what I thought I was "preparing for" was already very present and intimately a part of who his mother was. The thrill and hope that come with quickening, the difficult nights waiting for a test whose results aren't quite right, the discomfort, and impatience—all begin well before the date anticipated for the child's birth. So it is with those who are "preparing" for ordination or discerning their vocation in response to the gracious call or promptings of God. The first phrase of Mary's Magnificat expresses the disposition of many mothers as their children take form and grow within them. Likewise, it reflects the experience of many who seek to be faithful to God's call in their lives through a response that will require a commitment of their whole life and the attention of those who mentor and accompany the journey as their souls "magnify the Lord."

I have heard apologies from many mothers as the intensity of pregnancy grows for not being as attentive to the details and distractions of life. What I have come to understand is that a soul that magnifies the Lord is like a mother in the intensity of pregnancy focusing attention, energy, spirit, and hope, along with a bit of dread and fear, on the new life within her. Elizabeth provides the sanctuary and the hospitality for Mary.

Imagine what must have transpired with Elizabeth for Mary to be able to sort out the perplexing claims of God that had suddenly come upon her and turned her world upside-down and inside-out. Think of the wisdom and knowledge of the religious tradition Elizabeth shared to frame Mary's experience as the one who would fulfill the messianic hope. It is also clear that the future implications of what all of this would mean for God's people became articulate in Mary's sense of the greater importance of her calling. What it must have been like to mentor Mary through the wave of emotions that must have come with her realization! Consider the care and encouragement Elizabeth must have given for Mary to renew her commitment to the covenant of her people and the clear demands of that covenant in her own life. Try to raise in your own mind the list of questions Mary and Elizabeth struggled with in terms of the practical demands of raising the "Son of the Most High."

Elizabeth mentored Mary through the three months the Gospel reports they visited together. The young, perplexed, frightened, courageous Mary, who had fled from Nazareth, had found in Elizabeth a true mentor. The courage and faith Mary exhibited in embracing Gabriel's call and claim on her life were met in Elizabeth's encouraging, nurturing, framing, challenging, empowering, focusing, and attentive companionship. The immediate fruit of that relationship finds expression in Mary's *credo*—the Magnificat—embraced as one of the creeds of the whole church.

> My soul magnifies the Lord,
>> and my spirit rejoices in God my Savior,
> for he has looked with favor on the lowliness of his servant.
>> Surely, from now on all generations will call me blessed;
> for the Mighty One has done great things for me,
>> and holy is his name.
> His mercy is for those who fear him
>> from generation to generation.
> He has shown strength with his arm;
>> he has scattered the proud in the thoughts of their hearts.
> He has brought down the powerful from their thrones,
>> and lifted up the lowly;
> he has filled the hungry with good things,
>> and sent the rich away empty.
> He has helped his servant Israel,
>> in remembrance of his mercy,
> according to the promise he made to our ancestors,
>> to Abraham and his descendants forever. (Luke 1:46–55)

The place of the Magnificat in this first witness of Christian mentoring into vocation highlights the central place of theological understanding and articulation for these seminal partnerships. Mary discerned and clarified the meaning of her calling and affirmed the covenant that God had made with Israel and her own place within that covenant. Further, the articulation of Mary's theological claim in the sublime language of this cherished creed is imperative to the Gospel writer's purpose in relating this story. It claims *credo*—the articulate (reasoned) witness and understanding of what God is doing in light of the canon, traditions of the people, and experience—as a crucial task for the mentoring partners to undertake. It brings testimony, honor, and worship to what God has done and glorifies God's name in the community.

The Experience of the Disciples and the Early Church

The concept of Christian vocational mentoring must be conceived as part of the relationships intended to be experienced within *the whole community of the church*. Remembering the origins of mentoring in the collegiality of the disciples and the *koinonia* of the early church will help enrich the texture and ethos within which mentoring takes place.

The public ministry of Jesus Christ began with preaching the gospel of repentance and hope, coupled with the forming of a small, intimate group of disciples with whom he would share his ministry. Answering Christ's call to "Follow me!" the twelve were bound together with Jesus in mutual bonds of love and commitment. In the course of the three years they spent together, an ongoing model of learning, spiritual formation, and missional and evangelistic outreach developed. Jesus preached and taught; the disciples probed, questioned, witnessed, and needed guidance, clarity, rebuke, redirection, and invitation to further their discipleship. The central personality of the group was Jesus. He held them together and gave the group cohesion and purpose, and led them into the greater challenges of apostolic discipleship.[3] Despite Peter's objections, Jesus led them from the sublime setting of Galilee to confrontation in Jerusalem. Despite the arguments over power and succession (who will sit at the right hand and who at the left), Jesus offered them the way of the Cross.

When Jesus died on the cross, the group was leaderless and dispersed. It was only in confronting the risen Christ at the Resurrection that the group regathered to form the church at Pentecost. And this happened only with the infusion of the Holy Spirit, who led them to proclaim the gospel, heal, evangelize beyond the boundaries of their own horizons, and engage in the mission and work of Christ in the world.

In the letters of Paul we find the development of *koinonia*—a spirit of fellowship experienced in christocentric partnership such as that of Paul and Barnabas or Paul and Silas, as well as groups of believers united in the hospitality of the Holy Spirit. In the context of these small, informal partnerships and fellowships, the work of discipleship was formed and encouraged. It was in the intimacy of that group that scholars believe Christ's self-revealing work took place most fully.[4] Paul's letters concerned themselves with the internal life of Christian *koinonia*. These believers experienced an "unusual degree of intimacy," interacted with one another at a deep level, felt a powerful degree of cohesion as a group, and exhibited a self-perception that they were distinct from "outsiders" and the "world" due to their identity in Jesus Christ.[5] However, their sense of distinction in the world did not remove them from the world. The early church's mission was *in* and *to* the world. What distinguished them was their identity—an identity not found in the world but in Christ.

The first step in the process of discipleship was to turn from "the world," the "Gentiles," the "idols," and the past and to move into a community focused on the future promised by God in Jesus Christ by the power of the Holy Spirit. The community was the *ekklesia*, the church in a given locale. They were organized in enclaves like foreigners in a city.[6] By *ekklesia*, Christians of the first two centuries understood both the smallest expression of community, such as the apostles itinerating two-by-two, and the entire connexion of believers in Christ.

As we gather the character, substance, and methods of Christian vocational mentoring, reflection upon the life of Jesus with the disciples is the central example and source. The brief narrative above surveys only the ways in which Jesus related to the disciples and mentored them in their vocation. As mentors embrace their own role, the study of Jesus as a mentor to the disciples and those with whom he came in contact frames and forms the way in which the relationship should be practiced or must be flexible to meet the challenges of various personalities and dispositions. I think of Jesus' work with Peter as different from his mentoring of James and John. Peter was strong and trusted to be a rock; yet Jesus had to keep repeating and reframing the mission statement for his ministry, "Feed my sheep." James and John were tempestuous "sons of thunder" who needed to have their ambition curbed and redirected.

Jesus was open to reenvisioning his own understanding of the covenant of his ministry. His hospitality to the faith of the Syrophoenician woman reframed his own covenant of ministry, expanding his vision from the household of Israel to the whole inhabited earth. Jesus offered the canon as a living testament with the wisdom of a rabbi. The parable has been one of Jesus' chief offerings to my own ministry of mentoring and pastoring. I have found that stories and parables are very helpful because they invite mentees to "walk around" in narratives that may be similar to their own and hear their own experience framed in the faith story of another or in a parable. The ongoing steps of discipleship practiced in the relationships of the fellowship in Christ formulated the community and its mission. The retelling of the Jesus story led them to ask each other, "Lord, when was it that we saw you hungry and fed you?"

The retelling of Scripture and the stories of the tradition was an important root for community relationships, identity, and language. These stories informed the way in which mentors and mentees related. It was not simply to carry on received tradition or acquire certain skills to do the tasks of ministry. The expression of the language, stories, patterns of behavior emerging from retelling and conversing about Scripture, and the stories of the church's experience gave rise to assurance of what God expected of the church in its current and future mission, both in personal and in communal vocation.

One of the chief operating models out of which I work is as a collector of stories. As a pastor, I have the rare opportunity to visit with people who entrust me with the stories of their life's journey. Given the nature of my calling and the settings in which I meet most people, the story is usually the relating of a portion of someone's spiritual journey. I try to enable the telling of a person's story to become part of the divine story. As the leader of a local Christian community, I am also called upon to knit all the stories together and bring some meaning and direction in the service of ministry and mission for Jesus Christ. In this way, I believe that I am mentoring both individuals and the community in a method used by Jesus in relating parables.

I am awed by the width and depth and height of the faith, the commitment, the struggle, and the joy that is a hallmark of the stories of the people I have mentored through my ministry. I have also been struck by the loneliness many experience in their faith journeys. I was privileged to hear the heart of individuals' struggle and response to God in their own lives. Yet for many it was a solitary and secret part of their lives. I had often wondered how many others might benefit, were there a way intentionally to share the experience, wisdom, and struggle of such persons with others. So I began to ask permission to share these stories as part of the companioning of others in my one-on-one mentoring, as well as in group mentoring, where I encourage the sharing of stories. The promise of the blessing of "so great a cloud of witnesses" is manifold in the mentoring process.

At the moment, the official mentoring roles in The United Methodist Church are reserved for the ministry preparation process, leading either to certification as a candidate for ordained ministry or from the time of commissioning to ordination. However, it is my hope that these roles will be models of relationship for a life in ministry. In reflecting on the relationships Jesus fostered with the disciples and the intentional companioning of the early church, either in itinerant partnerships or in communities of *koinonia,* it seems irresponsible not to note the importance of mentoring relationships throughout the church, especially among the leadership. Signs of renewal within clergy covenant groups, cabinet discipleship covenants, spiritual renewal retreats, and the like are heartening. Even the adoption of "holy conferencing" as a model for renewing the annual gathering begins to revitalize The United Methodist Church along the lines of the models from which it sprang. John Wesley sought to reclaim the *koinonia* of the early church in the class meetings and the covenant of the circuit-riding preachers. The sense of isolation among the leaders of our church today, the struggle for authority and influence, the political realities of the way in which the machinery of the church operates—all seem to threaten to extinguish the spiritual bonds and covenants articulated at baptism and ignited in the hopes, dreams, visions, and willingness to make sacrifices to answer the call in ordination. It has caused some clergy attending workshops for mentor training to wonder whether the hospitality and *koinonia* I was inviting them to exhibit would give a false sense of what the covenant of ministry *really* was.

This concern found expression in an experience I had with a bishop who had a formative influence on the mission of the denomination. I was privileged to work very closely with him on a mission and justice project during the last days of apartheid in South Africa. I came to know the bishop's deep faith in Christ that birthed his commitment to mission, his passion for justice, and his vision for the way in which the church could utilize its vast resources in the activity of redemption and salvation. I sensed the bishop's frustration in trying to communicate and work with the bureaucracy of the church. It was clear that somewhere vocation had been consumed in the expectations of office. I listened, wondering what I should say to a bishop. He spoke about his isolation and loneliness as a human being and as a Christian. In that moment my own loneliness and isolation were named and touched. The vibrancy of my own call and vocation had been diminished by the daily demands of the pastoral office. But, like Elizabeth and Mary, we were "quickened" by the shared experience. What had been scheduled as a thirty-minute meeting stretched to ninety minutes as he invited me to walk with him in the heart of his ministry and to touch the core of his covenant of vocation. We met several more times after that, always in the "sanctuary of South Africa," away from the polity and the politics of annual conference life. Those times taught me that the *koinonia* of Christ, invited by our shared vocation, must be the heart of our relationships together in leadership of the church. The mentoring roles required by the preparation for ministry protocols are invitations to renew the quality and virtue of the relationships of the disciples with Jesus and the early church in Christ.

Methodist Ethos for Mentoring in the Class Meetings

The class meeting was the cornerstone of the Methodist revival. It brought together spiritual renewal, accountable discipleship, and empowering vocational discernment in vibrant relationship. It is instructive to the mentoring relationships, experienced either in one-to-one partnerships or in groups,[7] to absorb the ethos and character of the class meeting as part of the mentoring DNA of the Methodist movement. It is also a recovery of the experience of the disciples and the primitive church. The vocational aspect has been instructive in my own ministry when I have worked with laity who are trying to respond to God's call and claim through their own professions and occupations. Both group mentoring and one-to-one mentoring have been richly informed and blessed.

John Wesley called upon his understanding of the primitive *koinonia* to confirm his own vision of the structures of Methodism. His view of the early church yielded an intense image of the Christian fellowship, determined by voluntary commitment of those seeking to live out the Christian faith. He termed these gatherings *societies,* distinguishing them from Anglican practice, where "a church" referred largely to a parish whose members were determined by ancestral association and Christian catechism. In the parish church, the learning of catechism led to confirmation. By contrast, for Wesley, the concept of catechetical work was an ongoing commitment of Christian *koinonia,* which he saw reflected in the experience of the early church.[8]

Wesley drew up the "General Rules" for these meetings to guide in their discipline and development. The preamble to the Rules outlined the framework and thrust of these early meetings: seek the power of godliness; pray together; read the Word; exhort the Word; watch over one another in love; and help one another work out their salvation.

The Methodist experiment did not occur within a religious void. Wesley had drawn from similar experiments he encountered on the European continent and in England. The Moravian Peter Böhler, with whom Wesley was intimately familiar, advised the formation of the "Orders of a Religious Society Meeting in Fetter Lane." Wesley's Rules and those of Fetter Lane mirror each other.[9] Several other religious societies in London operated at the same time with similar thrusts.

The class-meeting experiment begun in 1739 was not a new phenomenon for John Wesley. His mother, Susanna, held meetings in the Epworth parsonage when John was a child. She also gave her sixteen children personal attention each week for education and spiritual counsel. This is an important model for contemporary mentoring. With the plethora of responsibilities and activities demanded of Susanna Wesley, she provided time and attention to each child every week. This made an indelible mark on the Wesley children. My church history professor, Earl Kent Brown, speculates that it was "Mother" Wesley who was the true source of the Methodist revival as well as the spiritual foundation for the class meeting. I would take it a step further: The spiritual and vocational formation and mentoring the Wesley children experienced with Susanna are exemplary and commendable as we today embrace the role of a mentor in the development of baptismal faith along with encouragement and empowerment for Christian vocation.

The proliferation of religious societies emerged in a culture that was dismal at best. The Church of England was in a spirit of lethargy and the great energy of the Dissenters who had brought Oliver Cromwell to power in the seventeenth century by the eighteenth century had diminished to very little. English society was perched on the brink of an explosion of industrialization that would establish a society that, in the half century following Wesley's death, Charles Dickens imaged in the stark fiction of *Oliver Twist, Bleak House, Great Expectations, Hard Times*, and the like. Wesley saw the great migration from a rural agricultural economy to industrialized urban sprawl, with increasing numbers of people moving to work and live in the coal mining country. The steam engine, the power loom, the spinning jenny, and the great pottery factories all were developed in Wesley's lifetime. Wesley's England was described as a time of "beastliness and debauchery," in which the moral character of England was "vitally decayed." The mass of the citizenry was perpetually unhappy, underemployed and poorly educated, and far from the ministry of the church. They "married and buried amongst themselves and often committed murders with impunity."[10]

The religious societies of the eighteenth century were the focus of revitalizing the personal experience of spiritual life in what was otherwise a laissez-faire approach to religious matters in the life of the mass of people. By their intensity of practice and experience and intimacy of meeting, the societies attacked the uncompromising individualism that was the isolating "ulcer of the age." The societies were the fertile field in which evangelical preaching took place; but it was not isolated to that single dimension of Christian proclamation of the Word. The Word, perhaps planted through preaching, was nurtured and made personal through the nurturing groups within the society. However, the Word was not to remain within the person or the *koinonia* but was specifically and practically to inform the life of a Methodist in the world. And the Methodist "practitioner" was held accountable for the way in which his or her spiritual commitments (*praxis*) were lived out in *practice*. The focus of the class meeting was to bring the member into a closer relationship with the living Christ and to seek his or her calling and place in the vocation of God.

The distinction between *praxis* and *practice* in the previous paragraph is deliberate. Let me briefly clarify what I understand by each term and how they relate to each other in the mentoring journey. Following the work of Tad Dunne, I use *praxis* to refer to the person's appropriation and internalization of knowledge of God, the teachings of Scripture, and the disciplines of the Christian life. *Praxis* has to do with the shaping of the person's interior life. *Practice*, on the other hand, refers to the myriad ways this accumulated wisdom finds expression in concrete acts and practices of ministry. However, *praxis* and *practice* are inseparably bound in the journey into vocation; they are indissoluble parts of a holistic spiritual practice. This dynamic interplay of *praxis* and *practice* must be a crucial focus of the work of mentoring. I discuss this topic more fully later in this chapter.

Accountability in the Mentoring Relationship

As the new protocols for the mentoring roles in the contemporary United Methodist entry into ministry have been established, the methods of accountability beyond the partnership have been difficult to define. Great concern has been expressed that any "reporting" beyond the mentor and mentee relationship would compromise the integrity and openness necessary for mentoring to be effective. I believe that this reveals an inherent mistrust in the institutional church and the ultimate purpose of mentoring. Clear lines of accountability beyond the intimacy of *koinonia* were essential to the "connexional" nature and strength of early Methodism.

It might be instructive to place our appropriation of the connexional model in the broader context of the ecology of early Methodism. We live in a world where privacy and secrecy inform the way we seek to protect what is done in mentoring partnerships. We call it "confidentiality." However, for United Methodists, confidentiality means the confidence not only of the immediate participants but also of the broader fellowship of the church with whom we seek to join in the vocation of Christ. Connexional accountability is an expression of the refining hospitality of a Holy Spirit–formed church.

51

Wesley established the practice of a quarterly examination of the members of the class meetings to see whether they were following the discipline and commitments of the covenant embodied in the General Rules. He wanted to support the work of the class leader to ensure that the integrity of the class meeting was maintained, given the intimate and important nature of the sharing and for the sake of the integrity of the Methodist movement. These were not loosely held rules. At the quarterly examination, Wesley, or one of the traveling preachers, would remove those who were lax in attendance and in practicing their personal spiritual disciplines or in their committed practice in the world.[11]

I am not saying that severity or termination of persons in vocational discernment or preparation for ministry is a good thing. Rather, I am pointing out that, for early Methodists, the focus was on accountability *beyond the mentoring partnership.* The commitment of the connexion and its examiners was to sustain the vitality of committed discipleship promised by the engagement of a dedicated mentoring leader and committed members. In exercising accountability, neither the examining circuit rider nor Wesley inquired about intimate details. The accounting lay in the integrity with which the process of vocational discernment and discipleship was engaged. Thus, when clergy mentors or candidacy mentors are asked by their colleagues for accountability, it should be seen in the spirit of the early connexion. It is a time to give an account of the attendance, attention, spiritual and formational discipline, and commitment to the covenants of the church. Wesley and the early Methodists understood these as keeping covenant and confidence with the fellowship of the connexion and the call and claim of Christ.

The key to the early Methodist *koinonia* was the desire to grow in relationship to God and in the confidence of faith. This was a doctrinal or devotional faith *and* vocational formation. The attention and commitment of each member were crucial components of the conviction and capacity to "work out the salvation" of each involved. There is evidence that the methods used by the class leaders to mentor those in their care went from sharing their experiences in the light of the gospel to strict catechesis, depending on the need of the partners. For early Methodists, the *koinonia* of the class meeting was one of the prudential means of grace. The mutual mentoring of spiritual growth and vocational empowerment was such a crucial part of the renewal movement that Wesley would not even pretend to give account of those societies that did not meet in class. "They hang on but a single thread."[12]

The touchstones for mentoring that I discuss in what follows reflect the ongoing work that has been set down in many of the journals of early participants in the class meetings. Members spoke of God's call and claim in their lives; they followed the requirements of the covenant of the General Rules and reflected on how those disciplines and commitments had worked themselves out in their lives. Clearly, the class meeting was inherently contextual. The weekly reflections, scriptural citations, and other resources melded together for use of the class were understood to have relevance and directly shaped daily experience. If testimony to the inner experience excluded any accountability of how it had been lived and witnessed in the world, it was the responsibility of the class leader and the other members to elicit the important discernment of the fruits of the spiritual life in works and outward behavior. The dynamic integration of the inner, spiritual life and its outward manifestation was imperative to maintaining the integrity of Christian vocation.

The mentoring practices in the class meeting are instructive for the interaction between mentor and mentee as they respond to the call of God in formation for ministry. It is not a speculative or exclusively interior exercise. Praxis must be understood and experienced in practice. The skill of the mentoring leader was to introduce Scripture, the resources of the Christian tradition, and the understanding of the spiritual life as efficacious for living one's vocation in the world. In the same way, the experience of living one's vocation in the world was grist for reflection and comprehending the Scriptures, tradition, and one's own spiritual formation in new and empowering ways.

In language that seems like an eighteenth-century precursor to the "What Would Jesus Do?" movement, the class meeting focused on discerning what "Jesus would have us do" in the situations class members confronted daily. The form of the weekly class meeting was very simple, with as many nuances and modifications as there were classes. At first, the meetings were stiff and formal, a requirement to participate as a Methodist. Most of the mentoring partnerships required in the United Methodist structure probably begin in the same manner. However, over time the class meetings emerged as intimate, "family" circles where the spirit and power of the intentional relationships of faith were fostered for the benefit of the *koinonia* and the redemption of the world through the empowerment of vocation.

It may be instructive for mentoring partnerships experienced in our contemporary setting to look at the structure of the early class meeting as a model for time together. The meeting was held in a place that the participants claimed as sacred. The time was also considered a specifically holy time when an appropriation of grace by the Holy Spirit was expected.

The leader/mentor would open the meeting with prayer and the singing of a hymn. The leader would then give testimony of his or her experience during the previous week in such a way that it invited the other members of the group to do the same. Following testimony, the leader would inquire about the experience of the members of the class—upon which members would tell their stories. It was not to be a particular confession or a set formula, but a general relating of the activity of the mind and spirit. The leader would then respond to the sharing and perhaps others would join in the response. If a member fell into sin, he or she was reproved and, if tempted, encouraged and comforted. If a member did well, he or she was exhorted to press on. Following the time of sharing, the final hymn was sung and the leader offered prayers of petition and other types of prayer based on the concerns of the group. He or she would then offer a final blessing.[13]

The Class Leader as Inspiration for Contemporary Mentors

The class leader played a pivotal role in the connexion of the class to the larger work of the society and the Methodist movement, as well as the ongoing sustenance of the class itself. The class leader had two meetings each week. The first was with the class itself. The class leaders shaped the agenda and flow of the meetings and were responsible for discerning the spiritual needs of the members, assimilating new members of the class, reactivating those who had fallen away, and going after those who had been put out of the Society. The class leader was the shepherd who went after the lost sheep. The second meeting was with the ministers and stewards to share the pastoral concerns that had emerged and to give an accounting of the financial contribution of the class toward the work of the society.

The role of the class leader began as a helper who would feed and guide the flock in the absence of the minister but grew into a permanent fixture in the organization of the movement. The class leader was the primary, personal caregiver—an extension of the pastoral ministry of the society. It is amazing to conceive of the kind of pastoral care that is done when each member of the community of faith is personally pastored on a weekly basis. Due to the importance of the class leader within the life of the Methodist movement, the brothers Wesley and their assistants were very careful about whom they picked and retained as class leaders. Leaders were selected because of their zeal for the work of the gospel, their capacity to share the love of God openly, their potential ability to discern the issues of the spirit that would be raised in the class, the skill to manage the class, and the potential for an ongoing dedication to the task for which they were selected and trained by Wesley and the assistants.

The task of the class leader was to

- witness to the spirit within
- master the Bible and theology as a student and a teacher
- discern and know the character and personality of the members
- enable the members to see their lives in the light of God's light
- deal with the hurts and joys in the experiences of members, rather than with general speculation
- shepherd the class
- remember that the leader is not an infallible judge, but one who is to watch over the members and who will be held accountable for them[14]

It is important to note that the class leaders met with the pastors or supervisors once a week for their own mentoring. In our contemporary experience of the mentoring role, those who administer the ministry preparation programs for the board of ordained ministry often complain that they have trouble getting people to be trained for the mentoring role, let alone meet together to be mentored themselves. The attention given to the mentoring and shepherding of class leaders in their work was as vital to the early Methodist connexion as the mentoring of the *koinonia* itself. Wesley and the other leaders were in constant attendance at the meeting of leaders to engage in mutual mentoring and spiritual refreshment.

Each setting where *koinonia* took place had a specific purpose in the life of the Methodist body of Christ; but they were interwoven and networked in connexion with one another. Each meeting encouraged engagement with the living Lord and looking after one another on the journey by knowing the love of God and growing in grace. Also, each meeting provided members with an opportunity to share in the ministry to which each is called and, at the same time, to integrate these experiences into the ministry to which the whole connexion is called. Therefore, the vitality of the body of Christ is reinforced in its ministry in the most personal form and most complete form all at the same time, with a network that enables those within the body who are itinerant to touch it in the whole as well as at a wide variety of personal levels.

The skill of the class leader/mentor was to keep three elements that framed and resourced mentoring and *koinonia* in a healthy balance—fellowship, companionship along the spiritual journey and discernment of the Christian experience, and spiritual disciplines—as well as maintain an environment in which a person could find encouragement for experimental Christianity (to follow the divine call and its practical implications in daily living). These three elements were melded and kept in some sort of balance in the experience of the class meeting. To lift up the Rules and diminish the other elements would be to risk dry formalism. Too heavy an emphasis on Christian experience would relinquish accountability (a fact that eventually led to the decline of the class meeting in the nineteenth century). And fellowship alone would not distinguish the class meeting from an afternoon tea.

The diaries of early Methodists focused on the friendships developed between spiritual companions. These were intimately linked to personal spiritual growth and experiences of God. Although the class meeting produced formative missional and social consequences through the witness of the members in their work, it is moving to read about the cherished personal experiences and support. It also helps give a sense of the texture of the meetings, for it opens them up to our own ability to enter into the experience.

As the class meeting experience gained in maturity and longevity, many within the movement came to see them as little companies of heaven. In his

A Plain Account of the People Called Methodists, Wesley notes, "It can scarce be conceived what advantages have been reaped from this little prudential regulation. Many now happily experienced what Christian fellowship of which they had not so much as an idea before. They began to 'bear one another's burdens', and 'naturally' to 'care for each other.' "[15] The testimony of many of my students and their supervisor/mentors, as well as my experience of good mentoring partnerships and church leadership teams, is that when they meet together they experience the time as having "done church." "Doing church" encompassed intentionally seeking the life of Christ in their own growth in grace, experiencing hospitality and encouragement to confess faults and failings, learning and redeeming the experience, and being aware that all this is done in the presence of the living God. The mentoring relationships and the *koinonia* fellowship can be a foretaste of the heavenly fellowship in the midst of the tumultuous world in which we find ourselves and to which each of us will return to fulfill our share in Christ's vocation.

Mentoring Into . . .

Mentoring relationships do not take place in a static environment. They are part of the journey of faith and the mission of God. Within the mentoring structures of The United Methodist Church, the journey is from call to certified candidacy (candidacy mentors), or from readiness to effectiveness (clergy mentors). The mentoring event may take place as a retreat or sanctuary, allowing an experience of Sabbath and reflection; but these occur in the midst of an active journey of transformation, renovation, and fulfilling vocational mission.

I chose the preposition *into* at the head of this section carefully to frame the relationship between the mentoring partnership and the vocation to which God has called us. We identify a person's particular calling within the general calling of the church, its members, and its leaders. "Into" gives us a sense of moving to the interior or the inside. The mentoring relationship must intentionally consider and move to the heart or core of the relationship a person has with God, to the vitality of the call as it shapes and forms a person's life and mission, as well as to the essence of the new identity "in" Christ that transforms and transfigures our very being as we grow "in" vocation.

"Into" also indicates a sense of taking up residence or taking owner-ship of identity. When I experienced my call, I turned to a good friend and used the expression, "I am going *into* the ordained ministry!" Her response was interesting, "That's not who *you* are. You're crazy!" Clearly, for her, instead of becoming a pastor, I was becoming crazy because of some sense of who I "really" was.

Christian vocation is not simply a set of skills or technical acuity. The test of Christian ministry is not predicated on skill sets and assessments, however helpful these may be to understanding gifts and the appropriate contexts and environments in which vocation will thrive. The path of a mentoring journey moves within the grace of God's transforming Spirit. It is essential to the work of "mentoring into vocation" that we affirm the transformation and empowering language that describes this journey.

One of my cherished memories of Sunday school was the day my mother served as a substitute. She brought along a poster with a pic-ture of our church on it with the saying, "I was glad when they said to me, 'Let us go to the house of the LORD!'" (Ps. 122:1). That lesson established the sense of "into" as a sense of inclusion: We were all invit-ed into God's house. Mentoring affirms the witness of God's inclusive call and covenant in the context of discerning the particular covenant of the mentee. We are baptized *into* the body of Christ. We are called *into* the covenant of ministry. We are ordained *into* the order of dea-cons or the order of elders. We are commissioned *into* the mission of God. We are summoned *into* worship and service. Each of these has dynamic meaning, but an essential piece that must permeate the jour-ney is the inclusion of God's grace.

Mentoring is about interiority. "Into" reminds us to stay focused there. It is concerned more with what is formed in the heart, mind, and soul than simply with evaluating practice. Tad Dunne helps us focus on interior as the core of the mentoring relationship.

> Practice deals with making or producing tangible, external effects. Praxis, by contrast, deals with how one conducts oneself, negotiates one's experiences and feelings. In other words, we engage in praxis before engaging in practice. Where practice is associated with practical-ity and know-how, praxis is associated with wisdom and discretion.[16]

Dunne moves further to look at the thought and prayer processes that inform choices. He also emphasizes the responsibility one takes for the choices, actions, and the use of gifts and what is produced from the interior life.

Before I responded to the call to ordained ministry, I was being trained as a theatrical director. My training focused primarily on the "method" style. It examined the interior life of an actor—the part of that interior life that related to and touched the role—so that he or she could play it with truth and transparency. I found myself looking for actors who had the talent and capacity to know themselves in such a way that they would allow themselves to be "touched" by the character they were to play and would pour themselves into the role until the role became theirs. As a director, I listened to the interior struggles and successes as the actor "grew into" the character. As director, my task was to affirm, test, challenge, and offer observations, alternatives, and options. I was also able to observe the interior decisions, commitments, and responses to the role as they were expressed in the action on the stage. The gifts of voice and movement were exercised, educated, rehearsed, and refined to be instruments of the praxis of the actor.

I contrast my approach as director with other directors, whose interest lay in perfecting the technique of the actor to get the desired product. These directors focused on the exercises and experiments in voice, physical character, movement, lighting, timing, and staging. I often said that to focus on practice is efficient and gets results. One of my teachers would brag that he could play a hand of cards backstage, put them down for his entrance, give a performance, and come off to join the game where he had left off. He had "put on" the character and worn it well. His technique was perfect. But he was unaffected by the role. It could be put on and taken off at will.

In contrast, for me, the method was about "becoming," about growing "into" the role so that it was part of who the actor was. One who had merely studied the technique would begin and end the character where the author confined it and the stage defined it. The method, on the other hand, had done the interior work of becoming so well that the actor could live the character before and continue to develop it after the containment of the script. This actor could go places that no one else could explore, because he or she had grown "into" the role. Like mentoring into Christian vocation, praxis is crucial to becoming. Effective practice follows from becoming. But more important, the mentee will have been directed, coached, guided, and nurtured to grow "into" the fullness of the vocation to which he or she is called and gifted and move far beyond what anyone, except God, could have ever imagined or thought.

Mentors are chosen and honored when they express the hospitality of God and the *koinonia* of the church as well as serve as stewards of the expectations and responsibilities of the *collegium* and, in practical terms, of the role a person's vocation will engage. In the context of the ministry preparation process in The United Methodist Church, the mentor sharpens the focus of the relationship and the process by exploring what the covenant of ministry to which God calls a person would mean when he or she is ordained *into* the order of deacons or the order of elders. While this is not the starting point of vocational mentoring, it is a crucial aspect. Candidacy mentoring is designed to explore the gifts, graces, and fruits that a person experiences, and helps the person discern the appropriate direction of his or her call in ministry. The phrase "in ministry" necessarily includes the particulars of what it will mean to be ordained *into* an order or move *into* vocation through a variety of occupations. The mentor stands as a source of experience, guidance, caution, reality testing, redirection, and wisdom.

We live in a period in history in which larger numbers of people have no sustained experience of the community of the church. They have not been immersed in its worship, teaching, fellowship, eschatology, or prophetic witness in society. Yet, in the providence and grace of God, they find themselves moved to enter seminary and pursue ministry or to begin attending church and become heavily involved in its life as a response to some encounter with God through the witness of a colleague, a neighbor, an acquaintance, or broadcast ministry. Pastors, seminary mentors, and advisors, as well as ministry preparation mentors, are discovering that they are mentoring a person both into Christian vocation and into the first steps of faithful discipleship and the rudimentary catechesis of the church. For many mentors, this is frustrating; they would like to assume that God calls those who are "cradle Christians." Denominations and boards of ordained ministry would like to assume that a person is a "cradle Methodist," with the culture and understanding of the church and denominational practices, traditions, and expectations as part of their spiritual and experiential DNA. Mentors, and the supporting networks of the church that attend upon those whom God has called, must recognize that the important work may begin not in the refinement of a call toward a certain order or office but rather in confirmation and catechesis as a way to welcome one whom God has called to vocation into the church.

In this good work, the mentor is a sign and presence of the church itself. In fact, the mentee may experience the mentor as the most formative expression of Christ that he or she has ever encountered. Mentors cannot assume that someone else in the church has fulfilled that ministry with the person who comes to be mentored into vocation. The mentoring partnership *is* the church. The mentoring partnership acknowledges being embraced and bound in the purposes of God and the vocation of Christ by the power and presence of the Holy Spirit.

Trust

The mentor is invested with the highest degree of trust, even though he or she is as frail and unworthy as any who might be consecrated for this ministry. The integrity of the church and the empowerment of the vocation of Christ are entrusted to the sacred relationship that one hopes will form between a mentor and mentee. Mentoring in the United Methodist ministry preparation process is not simply an administrative task of screening or orientation or apprenticing or skill assessment and development. It is fundamentally a trust bestowed upon the mentor for the care and shepherding of a child of God in the fulfillment of his or her baptismal faith. Further, the church entrusts its sanctity, the care of its people, and the fulfillment of its mission to the dedicated work of a mentor with the mentee.

I am frequently bemused that annual conferences and districts have trouble finding mentors among their orders. It reminds me of the vexing problem local churches often have in finding Sunday school teachers and the pathetic plea from the pulpit or from students for someone to come forward to teach. This is usually followed by the wringing of hands and scratching of heads, wondering why children do not grow up to become an active and vital part of the church. I often challenge the leaders of local churches to be the most active teachers and learners themselves as a sign of the importance of the investment necessary to teach the next generation.

I believe that the same is true of the leadership of the church. We must ask ourselves whether those who are leaders and the most gifted should be deployed primarily in the administration of the church—meaning the management of its systems and processes—or whether they should make the mentoring of persons divinely called into the vocation of Christ their focus. I look to the example of John Wesley, who was not only a master organizer and preacher but who also reserved a large portion of his ministry to mentoring through the class meeting or in his work with the circuit riders. A small treasury of that work is preserved in letters, journal entries, and the descriptions of those Methodists and others who benefited from the trust that Wesley assumed was incumbent upon him—the same trust given to each of us who have been entrusted, under orders, with the leadership of the church.

Courage

It takes courage to be a mentor. Courage is one of the unspoken yet essential virtues of those who engage this work. If we are honest, we will acknowledge that it takes courage to speak in a way that assumes knowledge of God and God's way, with the intention of helping in the transformation God has called forth. It takes courage to help someone make decisions about God's intentions for his or her life in light of the ultimate fulfillment of God's reign. Mentors are called upon to be future oriented. Leading *into* the future is the courageous act of moving oneself and another person onto a way and to a place that he or she may not have gotten by himself or herself. Mentors exhibit the courage of this kind of faith not only for themselves but also by encouraging another. Further, mentoring is not about simply advising another person or generating options or possibilities. It is about accompanying a mentee on a formative journey that has implications for both the mentee and the mentor through the impact their journey has on the body of Christ of which they are a part and for which they have pastoral care and responsibility.

However, mentors do not control what is happening in the transformation or vocation of the mentee in their care. The role of the mentor is much like Paul's description of the church as an earthen vessel (2 Cor. 4:7). The mentor provides a "container" or a "vessel" within which the transformation can take place. It is the "molding" and transforming work of the Holy Spirit that is the imperative focus of the relationship. In many ways mentors are the shores of the Wadi Jabbok that witness Jacob wrestling; at times, perhaps, they are the figure with whom Jacob wrestles. Mentors are often active witnesses to the limps and transformations born of wrestling (Gen. 32:22–32). Or consider patient and healing Ananias, who mentors Saul through his post-Damascus calling and blindness. Ananias is filled with divinely bestowed courage to look beyond Saul's reputation as an evil persecutor of Christ's followers and to lay hands on, baptize, and be present in the days when Paul gains clarity about his vocation (Acts 9:10–19).

Mentors must exhibit the courage to remain and travel with their mentees in their journey. They must also have the gift of wise encouragement. While itinerating among the districts of the Methodist Church of Southern Africa, holding workshops on clergy mentoring, I was blessed to spend a day at Addo Elephant Park in the Eastern Cape. My hosts, themselves clergy mentors, took my wife and me through the park in a small car. Charmaine was driving. She was from the seminary in Pretoria and not as familiar with the park as Peter, who sat behind her. It was a glorious day. Ostrich, kudu, zebra, birds of every kind, and warthogs were in abundance, along with the magnificent elephants. As we came over the crest of a hill, four large Cape buffalo, with great horns and intimidating faces, confronted us. Charmaine brought the car to a stop. This was a difficult moment. We could back way up and return the way we came. Or we could deal with what was before us. Peter acted as Charmaine's mentor.

"Ease a little closer," he said, which she did. Both she and Peter became more attentive to the disposition of the animals. I snapped photos and hoped that my hosts knew what they were doing. The four beasts stared at us.

"Just a little closer," Peter said. Charmaine brought the car to a closer range. The buffalo were big. Three of them wandered off the road, leaving one to keep watch on us. "Just a little closer; perhaps they are leaving and we can get along." Charmaine advanced the car another little way. Charmaine narrated each advance. She was clear that she was still the driver, and she let us know on what basis she was making the decisions. She tested Peter to make sure that he knew something about the behavior of the buffalo and that his judgment had credibility. She was clear that the car could move rather quickly in reverse.

The three buffalo returned. Their parliament was over. They stared at us—intently.

"Charmaine, do you think that buffalo paw at the ground *before* they attack?" Peter had reached the boundary of his knowledge and the ability to encourage any further. He was clear that it was now Charmaine who would not only make the decisions but also lead us. And Peter trusted her fully to do it. He put his hand on her shoulder in a gentle gesture of commissioning and trust. Charmaine studied the buffalo. She was fully attentive to the challenges ahead and the responsibility around her and us.

The buffalo moved off the road, and we were on our way.

Dedicated companionship, acute understanding of responsibility, assessment of where the future would lead and what challenges lay ahead, courage, wisdom, knowledge, encouragement, understanding of personal limits and boundaries of knowledge, and blessing a mentee—all were present in those ten tense yet wonderful minutes of mentoring. In many ways, mentors must be aware that the reality of their work has the same exigency even if it is experienced in the relative safety of an office, or over coffee.

Courage is the mentor's willingness to be both an accompanying pastor and a prophet and a priest. Mentoring *into* vocation is not simply to accompany a person on the journey that he or she has charted or to accommodate a person to an orientation and entry process of the church. It is to claim the mantle and discern the appropriate sifting of the roles of prophet, priest, and pastor. It takes courage to intervene in the development of a person's call, to offer tests or challenges of refinement that may lead to redirection and, perhaps more accurately, to fulfillment. It is to assume the faithful task of articulating the work of the Holy Spirit.

A college student sought me out for mentoring. It was clear that he had passion to respond to the call of God in his life. He was convinced that pastoral ministry was the way he should respond to that call. In our conversations, it became clear that he was most comfortable with study and teaching. He wanted to focus his efforts there. He touched lightly on his concerns about hospital visits and preaching as well as his distaste for administration. However, he kept coming back around to the teaching and study of Scripture. It was evident to me that he was articulating his call and how he would live it out vocationally. However, his clarity remained focused on pastoral ministry in the local church. I had two choices. I could wait until recommendation time and point out that the areas he feared needed further work, thus pushing the issues to some other process and engendering further frustration for the system of entry and for my mentee. Or I could walk with him through this part of the journey. I invited him to join me in the emergency room in the local hospital. I made arrangements to take a chaplaincy rotation. He rose to the occasion and responded to the patients with tenderness and support. He clearly had gifts. But our time together in the emergency room prompted him to reflect intentionally on how best to use his gifts. Actually being "in the role" with a trusted companion clarified and enabled him to reach beyond the "expected" response to God's call. It allowed him to examine his response and to explore a variety of paths. The courage we took was to move a little outside the box of mentoring defined as counseling and to walk together through a refining moment of clarity. It was to have faith that, as a mentor who had listened deeply, I could discern the place of the refiner's fire accurately and that walking through it and beyond it would be an empowering experience of covenant and vocational direction. He was able to name "teacher" as his identity and not as one of the many responsibilities of a pastor. He was able to claim teacher as a Christian vocation, even though his passion was not to teach in a place where he would be known as a Christian teacher (such as a seminary). He is now a very successful teacher and advisor to young people who are at the age of making critical decisions about their own futures.

It is important to know the boundaries and context of the mentoring relationships in which we may find ourselves. We should never exercise courage and move outside the box for its own sake but always in response to the work of the Holy Spirit in the relationship. Some relationships may not be appropriate for transcending the bounds of the conference chamber, such as candidacy mentoring. The establishment of trust, confidence, and mutual, personal investment is paramount for discerning the appropriateness of the kind of mentoring exemplified in the emergency room.

Mentors may also have to exhibit the courage to challenge power and authority in the course of their mentoring relationship. This is exemplified for us in the sweep of the narrative of the Hebrew Bible. The direct mentoring of God and God's people waned in the narrative with the rise of the monarchy. With the monarchy came the role of prophet. It was the prophet who mentored the monarch on behalf of God. I will not dwell long on the difference between false prophets and those we embrace as the witness and "seers" of God. Suffice it to say that it is important for people of power to surround themselves with prophetic mentors who are able to say more than yes and simply justify the thinking, words, and actions of the one in power. Among the brilliant examples that illustrate various methods of prophetic mentoring, the relationship of the prophet Nathan to King David stands out. Their relationship expresses the necessary companionship of a colleague who possesses the faithful courage and steadfast commitment to the one in power to offer himself as mentor. Consider Nathan's style in leading David to discover himself in light of his sending Uriah to his death so that David might steal Bathsheba (2 Sam. 12). Recall the courage to remind David that Yahweh preferred to live in a tent rather than in a house of cedar. The fruit of Nathan's mentoring was the renewal and reestablishment of Israel's covenant with God through David and his descendants (2 Sam. 7).

I am taken with Isaiah of Jerusalem's mentoring of King Ahaz. I am especially drawn to the conduit of the upper pool on the highway to the Fuller's Field (Isa. 7) when the destruction of Judah is imminent and the pressures of leadership threaten to compromise Ahaz's faithful dispensation of his office. "Take heed, be quiet, do not fear, and do not let your heart be faint" (7:4). The mentor Isaiah listens to the familiar words of the ancient covenant God has made and trusts them in the current crisis: the poetic retelling of the sacred story, the offering of a meaning-filled sign in the child Emmanuel, the contextual remembrance of the promise and hope of a righteous remnant, and encouragement for Ahaz to remain faithful to his vocation as a monarch whose first responsibility is to God for the leadership of the people. Isaiah's mentoring words are still wisdom, hope, and promise for the contemporary church. Isaiah introduced

Emmanuel, the sign of God with us. The Christian mentor continues to be that sign for us today.

I have deeply appreciated the several pastoral teams I have been blessed to lead. The fellowship and mutual covenant of leadership are expressions of and profound experiences in Christian *koinonia*. Further, the mutual mentoring that I have attempted to foster has empowered a fruitful and fulfilling journey in Christian vocation. However, it was important for me to be aware of the power dynamics within the collegial relationships. No matter how much we worked at mutuality and egalitarian practices, it was clear that I was the pastor, with all of the issues of power and authority that the office entails. For fruitful mutual mentoring to occur within the structures of power, it is essential to create an atmosphere in which observations, wisdom, counsel, and correction—even rebuke—can be faithfully offered and received with the anticipation that one's vocation may be changed, enhanced, refined, and more faithfully formed, even if the words are difficult. Diane Ladd was the first member of a team I worked with to teach me the importance of this kind of courage. In fact, it was her mentoring me *into* vocation that framed the importance of mentoring, both lay and clergy, in my own ministry.

The weekly meeting of the leadership staff had begun to wind down. Diane had walked us through the needs and plans of the Christian Education area she directed. As her report neared a close, she looked directly at me and said, "You think you're a good preacher, don't you?" Somehow, I got the feeling I was in trouble and a dreaded truth was about to be revealed about something I cherished in my quiver of gifts. "Well, that you may be; but your greater gifts are in your counseling of people in finding their way in the work of God. That's where you need to be spending your time!"

I was speechless (much like Zechariah's being struck mute, an embarrassing moment for a preacher) and confused. I wasn't quite sure what it meant to have the one thing I cherished as my identity and primary gift—being a preacher—diminished and a role I didn't even have a name for lifted up as formative in my relationship with that congregation. The look on my face must have been quite expressive, as Diane asked whether she had offended me. I was at a loss for words to accurately express how I felt. I felt confused yet affirmed at the same time. She did not retreat but waited patiently.

Over the next weeks and months, Diane and the staff mentored me in finding the words and concepts that framed what she had opened in that meeting of *metanoia*. It was a time in which they mentored me in naming and claiming the gifts they saw in me. They walked with me in examining how to rearrange the focus of my ministry in the exercise of my daily schedule and empower the staff and lay leadership to be effective partners. It was that courageous moment that led to a focus in that church and subsequent appointments on vocational discernment and empowerment as the framing principle of pastoral leadership. That encounter led to my doctoral work, my work with seminary students, and my work with the mentoring programs of the church and the myriad persons who were seeking to find their life's labor bound up in the vocation of Christ. I am deeply grateful to colleagues in *koinonia* who patiently mentored me in order to help me assess my gifts in new contexts and fulfill my vocation while empowering the vocation of others through effective leadership. The courage of a collegial mentor to speak the truth to one whose temporal power is greater is an imperative God-given gift and is exemplified in the prophets.

Most of us assume that the process of mentoring into ministry places the mentor in a position of power over a mentee. This is true, if it is assumed that mentoring into ministry is primarily a screening mechanism. However, in the truest experience of mentoring, even in the entry process, the *mentee* may be the one exercising far more power and authority than the mentor. I was privileged to mentor an ambassador from a foreign government in assuming his role in the foreign ministry of a superpower. He was used to the confidence of his own government and the navigation of authority and diplomacy needed to dispatch his duties in the diplomatic corps in a high-profile position during a time when the world was attending the activity in the capital to which he was deployed.

During his time as ambassador, he experienced a call to the preaching ministry; and I eventually became his mentor as he prepared for ministry. His culture, his station, and his position had given him a great sense of personal authority and power over other people. His theological reading of Scripture reinforced a very directive, monarchical right incumbent upon the pastoral office. While I respected his experience and effectiveness as an ambassador, it was clear that his gifts for pastoral ministry were overshadowed by the somewhat intimidating power he exercised in our time together and by his expectations. We were under a time constraint due to the deadlines of the ministry process. Given the integrity expected of a Christian mentor, I could not simply move him along. He was not used to the direct evaluation I was to give him. It was not part of his experience, given the position he had held in his government. I had to stop the clock on the process and give a difficult evaluation. I completed my evaluation by affirming the gifts of an ambassador but yearned that they might be in the spirit and nature of Christ and not a reflection of the powers and principalities of this world.

My concern was that I would offend him or his culture. I was also aware that, given the priorities the church had for persons who would be treasured as leaders, his profile would be more than welcome. "No one has ever spoken to me in this manner before," he said. I was concerned about where this might go. "I will not complete the process on time. That is a problem." He lowered his head. There was long silence filled with an energy that I couldn't distinguish. "I had wanted to be ordained to the office of pastor. What will I need to do to be an ambassador for Christ?" It was a question I hadn't expected. I had braced myself for a difficult response, not an inviting one.

"I believe we should start by your showing me how you were an ambassador. That is your expertise." We spent a year together, teaching each other and learning from each other. He showed me his diplomatic talent and allowed me to see it from the inside. I came to understand that successful diplomacy knows the limits of power, the art of persuasion, use of language, as well as an acute sense of the needs and vulnerability of other nations. Those gifts were offered, claimed, reformed, and refined for ministry. The fruit of that journey, postponed in the official process for a year and at a dear cost, was a detour into the vineyard of vocation; and the fruit has come in abundance.

Transformation as the Work of the Holy Spirit, Not as the Design of the Mentor

Mentors help identify gifts, elements of personality, understandings of the faith, necessary gifts, and the like that will form and identify vocational possibilities and directions. But a mentor must never believe that he or she is doing the forming. Nor can the mentor control what God, through the Holy Spirit, will do in the life of the mentee. Transformation is the gift and work of God. The mentor must offer the mentee courage and encouragement and help him or her articulate the definition of what God is doing.

Christian Mentors—Friends in Christ

Pastor Norman Bent welcomed us as a delegation of Witness for Peace to Nicaragua during the Contra War. His words have stayed with me for the twenty-some years since I first heard them. "Welcome, friends! I don't mean that in some fleeting and superficial way. Nor do I mean it as a greeting to someone I have known since childhood and will share my secrets with until I die. I greet you as a friend, because you are clearly friends as Jesus described a friend." He went on to quote John 15:12–17:

> This is my commandment, that you love one another as I have loved you. No one has greater love than this, to lay down one's life for one's friends. You are my friends if you do what I command you. I do not call you servants any longer, because the servant does not know what the master is doing; but I have called you friends, because I have made known to you everything that I have heard from my Father. You did not choose me but I chose you. And I appointed you to go and bear fruit, fruit that will last, so that the Father will give you whatever you ask him in my name. I am giving you these commands so that you may love one another.

We were in a dangerous place, with the war raging around us. We were going into the heart of the place where the two factions were marshaled to face off. Yet this Moravian welcomed us in order for us to be friends. We were friends because we were friends in Christ, seeking to expand the bounds and depth of our love and care to the *campesinos* of the border regions of Nicaragua, who were the targets of war. Pastor Bent became our mentor in those days, encouraging us to know Christ in the experiences and friendships he led us to make. In conversation with him, I came to understand that friendships made in Christ, as the Gospel passage indicates, are not transitory. They are held in the eternal providence and purpose of Christ and are an indelible mark and sign of Christ that, as Pastor Bent termed it, "cross-pollinates" so that the friendship gives each the ability to bear fruit for Christ.

In Jalapa I met a woman who was well along in her pregnancy. She was in a small room that had been turned into the village memorial to those killed or missing in the war. She was lighting a candle for two of her children who had been killed while harvesting coffee. I also learned that her husband had been killed. I asked her how she could bring another child into a world filled with this kind of violence that stripped her of everything. I wondered aloud with her whether she was afraid that this child might also be taken from her. She reminded me that life is about hope. Without hope, there is no life. The child she was carrying *was* hope. She reminded me further that we had come as "friends" because we shared her hope and were willing to stand on the border and give our lives for the peace of her country. On the way home, Pastor Bent reminded me that I may never see that woman again or know what happened to her child; but our brief friendship would bear fruit in our lives.

Mentors are friends to mentees in the spirit of Christ.[17] They are called to give themselves in the kind of friendship described in the passage from John Pastor Bent shared with us and exemplified in his relationship to us. Mentors are friends in that they give themselves to the mentees, not reserving their wisdom, attention, creativity, prayer, advice, counsel, or energy. They are called to join in Christ's love for the person entrusted to their care. At times, I heard or was told by those seeking candidacy that they experienced indifference in either the appointment of a mentor or in the mentor's responsiveness to them. The United Methodist Church has adopted the important role of a mentor. With that choice to adopt this role, the denomination has assumed the responsibility for ensuring that its mentors be the kind of friends to whom Jesus gave this commandment and commission. Laying down one's life, searching, finding, revealing, and claiming the work and purposes of God in the formation of Christian vocation—all require the attention that the love God desires we have for one another.

We remember what Jesus said of both mentor and mentee, "You did not choose me, but I chose you." Mentor and mentee forge a friendship in their chosenness and in their attentive humility to foster the gifts of love that will bear fruit that will last.

Mentoring Skills Encouraged in Contemporary Models

Just as the adoption of the classical term *mentoring* for use in describing a relationship fundamentally formed for the church in Christian relationship, so some of the skills focused in a variety of related roles may invite specific methods within the mentoring journey. Several church sources have advocated the idea of a variety of *support professionals* to accompany and enhance the effectiveness of ministry. In many ways this mirrors a secular model of collecting expertise and consultants with specific specialties. In some circumstances that may be helpful. However, it seems prudent, efficient, and effective for mentors to be able to sift together the various skills as part of their companionship and relationship with the mentee. After all, we are not looking primarily for expertise but for ways in which faithful discipleship and Christian vocation can be fulfilled.

Some in the church have adopted *coaching* strategies from the world of business and sports. The role of the coach is to increase skills and to inspire and motivate. Teamwork and giftedness are shaped toward excellence. Coaches look for talent and try to find strategies to develop it. Confrontation and strategy are important skills for a coach. Many times coaching is important to develop the preparation and delivery of a sermon, use the gifts of a particular person, and develop people to their potential. Administration strategies, deployment of people, and the formation of teams to accomplish certain goals may require the mentoring skills of a coach.

Apprenticeship is a model that must be used with great care. This model has to do with passing on a craft from a "master" to a "novice." The emphasis is on hands-on, one-to-one work. Much of the work of the apprentice style is focused on "how-to." Formation, *praxis,* theological understandings, and ways of doing things in practice are passed on from the master to the novice. The mentor is given the constant responsibility of evaluation and determining when the novice has completed his or her training and is ready to do ministry on his or her own.

From time to time in my mentoring relationships, a mentee would ask me to show him or her how to do one thing or another in ministry. One student asked whether he could shadow me for a week or so to see how I organized my day and responded to various crises, interruptions, and the like. This was actually fruitful for both of us, as the questions raised caused me to reflect more fully on what I was doing.

The teaching profession develops a relationship that places the mentee in a dual role: the student of the mentor exercises the role of "demi-teacher," with a selected group of students under the final care of the supervising teacher. This is similar to the model used in student placements for seminary students and a resident site supervisor. The relationship is formulated to observe the student teacher or seminary student intern; to assess, coach, demonstrate, model, and guide professional acuity and development. The *praxis* skills are effective decision-making while practicing this craft. This is made possible because the teacher is always present to activate reflection as the work is unfolding and to monitor decision-making processes as well as the formational foundations that inform those decisions. The relationship's trajectory is to develop a collegial relationship between the teacher and the student intern or student teacher. The relationship also involves frequent and consistent times of confidential reflection, gifts identification, and skill-building. The goal is for the student teacher or seminary student intern to be effective when he or she becomes a pastor or classroom teacher.

As a mentor of seminary interns, I discovered that to be able to have ongoing reflections as events unfold and to mirror and compare reactions and issues of *praxis* require a dynamic relationship. Two poignant memories come to mind. One involved sharing a prison visitation with Karin for her first visit behind the wall; the second concerned working with Brad in a time of crisis. In both cases these seminary student interns were absorbing a flood of data and stimuli. I had the advantage of asking them what was going on in real time. They were able to articulate and formulate what was happening in their emotions; what was swirling around in their heads; decisions they thought they needed to make in response to the situation; and the biblical/theological/spiritual metaphors, images, and frameworks that informed their experience. While intense and exhausting, the exercise was vital to their development as "theological agents" (a term they adopted for themselves), functioning as they were out of the resources of the faith brought to bear in the immediate practice of ministry. What I learned from them is that to function out of a framework of Scripture, tradition, theological imagination, and spiritual awareness is to be marinated in the resources of the faith and to exercise the mentee's availability and capacity to inform reflective action in real space and time. Such a posture also requires the capacity for the mentoring partnership to be self-reflective and self-critical in the retreat to the mentoring "sanctuary" so that *praxis* and practice are open to God's reproach and refinement and not simply the acquisition of knowledge and strategies justified by repair to the proverbial axioms of the faith.

The term *supervision* has been used in seminary field education for a long time to denote the mentoring relationship. The notion of supervision in field education is distinct from supervision in The United Methodist Church nomenclature. For United Methodists, the function of the district superintendent and bishop, along with that of the board of ordained ministry, is supervisory in nature. They have to do specifically with the juridical function of assessment, evaluation, direction, and profession. In many ways the distinction between the functions of supervision and the role of the mentor is important in the way in which the institution of the church has developed its structures and expectations of leadership functions.

From the way the church has distinguished the functions of supervision from mentoring, it is clear that supervision requires evaluations that determine job security, appointments, and professional "rewards." The mentoring relationship has been conceived to "protect" vocational discernment and empowerment from these mechanisms of official denominational power. However, it is important to probe the rich meaning of the words *supervision* and *superintendent*, for it helps to clarify the relationship between the functions of mentor and those of the superintendent/supervisor. Embedded in the title and function of the superintendent/supervisor is the challenge of keeping the larger vision and greater intention of the institution through the administrative functions he or she performs. In their interaction with those in their care, superintendents/supervisors constantly evaluate the work of these persons in the context of this larger vision. To separate mentoring from supervision, as we are wont to do today, indicates a lack of the critical relational elements of trust and holistic pastoral engagement on behalf of the superintendent. I look forward to the day when the functions of supervision and mentoring are not seen as discrete and in tension with each other. I yearn for the day when the role of the mentor and the role of the supervisor are mutually reinforcing in the divinely commissioned ministry of nurturing a person into vocation.

Christian Mentoring as Harbinger of Renewal

Above we set out the role of the Christian mentor as framed by the scriptural record, the traditions of the church, my and others' experiences as mentors, and the core of the Methodist revival of the church. United Methodists simply must cherish the development of the mentoring role as a sign of renewal in the church as it seeks to express the vocation of Christ. Its intentional attentive relationship in Christian friendship and discipleship for the purpose of responding to Christ's call and claim in vocation redeems the life of the individual and the fellowship of the church and its witness in the redemption of the world.

The diaries of the early Methodists are a benediction on the relationships that our contemporary nomenclature has adopted as mentoring. These writings have extraordinary implications for the formation of vocation, the fervent engagement of Christ's mission in the world, the faithful discipleship of the church, and the work of justice. These diaries were developed, discerned, encouraged, and inspired in the quality and commitment of the experience of the mentoring partnership.

Joseph Nightengale observed the commitment of one of the leader/mentors of the early Methodists.

> [The leader expressed his] joys, and his sorrows; his hopes and his fears; his conflicts with the world, the flesh, and the devil; his fightings without and his fears within; his dread of hell, or his hope of heaven; his pious longings and secret prayers for the prosperity of the church at large, and for those his brothers and sisters in class particular.[18]

William Holder was edified by Mr. Walton's leadership and mentoring on the first day they met together. Their experience clearly reflects the relationships forged in meetings very much like the relationships invited in mentoring. Holder wrote in his diary:

> This day we spent about two hours in close fellowship together, we found great freedom to speak our minds to each other, and hearts were

so knit together that each could have put the other in [his] bosom, though, had not seen each other before; does not [that] prove the peculiarity of the love of God, and, also how great the Lord is delighted in the communion of his people, for what beside could have knit us together. When he told me how he was when he first felt deliverance from all sin. I believed what I experienced three, or four years past, was the same work; Oh! How did my heart burn within me, for I felt my soul greatly inclined to see it again, and believe it near.[19]

The quickening of the Holy Spirit at work in the calling to deliverance and salvation is clear in this passage and many others in the early Methodist records. The engagement of relationship in the class meeting led to discerning and empowering Christian vocation in the world. Reclaimed from Christian antiquity, modeled in countless biblical relationships, enjoyed by covenant partnerships and communities across the history of the church—the invitation to relationships now termed *mentoring* promise to quicken the vocational commitment of the church, its members, and its leaders that "[our] soul will magnify the Lord and [our] spirit will rejoice in God our savior."

Notes

1. "Wake, Awake, for Night Is Flying," in *The United Methodist Hymnal* (Nashville: The United Methodist Publishing House, 1989), 720, stanzas 1 and 2.

2. *The Book of Discipline of The United Methodist Church—2008* (Nashville: The United Methodist Publishing House, 2008), paragraph 349.2.

3. Charles William Cook, "The Disciplined Small Group in the Local Church" (Diss., Perkins School of Theology, 1982), 41.

4. Joyce Neville, *How to Share Your Faith without Being Offensive* (New York: Seabury, 1979), 75.

5. Wayne A. Meeks, *The First Urban Christians: The Social World of the Apostle Paul* (New Haven: Yale University Press, 1983), 74, 75.

6. Wayne A. Meeks, *The Origins of Christian Morality: The First Two Centuries* (New Haven: Yale University Press, 1993), 212.

7. The clergy mentor and candidacy mentor pieces of the process were con-

ceived as one-to-one experiences. However, some annual conferences or districts do not have the capability or resources to accommodate this model and have adopted group-mentoring models.

8. Ted Campbell, *John Wesley and Christian Antiquity* (Nashville: Kingswood Books, 1991), 86.

9. David Lowes Watson, *The Early Methodist Class Meeting* (Nashville: Discipleship Resources, 1985), 197.

10. Oscar Sherwin, *John Wesley, Friend of the People* (New York: Twayne Publishers, Inc., 1961), 29; and Larry O. Tingle, "The Wesleyan Class Meeting: Its History and Adaptability for the Twentieth Century Church" (Diss., Wesley Theological Seminary, 1984), 29.

11. Watson, *Early Methodist Class Meeting*, 105.

12. John Wesley, *The Works of John Wesley* (Grand Rapids, MI: Baker, 1979), 2:512.

13. *The Lives of Early Methodist Preachers: Chiefly Written by Themselves* (London: Wesleyan Conference Office, 1866), 1:190; 3:70.

14. Watson, *The Early Methodist Class Meeting*, 99–102, 219.

15. John Wesley, *The Works of John Wesley* (Nashville: Abingdon, 1989), 9:262.

16. Tad Dunne, *Spiritual Mentoring: Guiding People through Spiritual Exercises to Life Decisions* (San Francisco: HarperSanFrancisco, 1991), 14ff.

17. For an important discussion of friendship as a theological principle of ordained ministry, see Edward C. Zaragoza, *No Longer Servants, but Friends* (Nashville: Abingdon, 1999).

18. Watson, *Early Methodist Class Meeting*, 95–96. I include these quotations because they exhibit early Methodists' attention to and hope in the whole work of the church expressed in the vitality of the relationships forged in the *koinonia* of the class meeting and the mentoring relationship the leader had to its members. They are touching in their intimacy and commitment to both the members and to Christ.

19. This is an excerpt from the manuscript diary of William Holder, transcribed by Prof. Tom Albin.

Chapter 3

VOCATION WATERED IN BAPTISM

Brad had abundant gifts for ordination as an elder. His field education placement was at the church where I was the senior pastor. His vibrant and articulate faith infused his skills as he practiced ministry among the members of the congregation. I also had the privilege of meeting with him weekly to engage in the sacred task of mentoring. The integration of classroom work and study in Scripture, theology, ethics, history, and the practice of ministry courses was integral to our time together. Brad's *praxis* was drawn from the riches of the tradition along with a deep and compassionate faith.

It was getting close to the time when Brad was to appear before the board of ordained ministry to be examined for ordination. He had asked me to read his papers. They were excellent and reflected accurately what I experienced in him. His autobiographical statement reminded me that he had received his call to ministry before his sixteenth birthday. He had been looking forward to ordination ever since. Having been part of the board of ordained ministry process as well as chairing the district committee process, I was aware that any number of factors could make the interviews difficult and the outcome disconcerting. So I asked Brad what would happen if he were to fail to receive an affirmative answer from the board and was denied ordination or were to continue as a candidate and be asked to reapply next year. It was a difficult question; but I thought that it was better for me to ask it than for him to encounter it at the other end of a juridical decision communicated in a long-distance phone call.

Brad sat silently. He had received the question genuinely. He knew that I had every confidence in his call and his gifts. The difficult experiences of his classmates when they had encountered the board were legion in the conversations at the seminary refectory. The idea that a luminary in the eyes of the seminary community would be turned down by the board might have been unfathomable, but it was not outside the realm of experience. We sat together in silence for a while. I wondered whether my question had gone too far. We prayed together and went about our day—until Sunday morning worship. Brad was scheduled to preach.

The chancel was configured so that I sat behind Brad as he stood in the pulpit. After a brief introduction, he said, "A friend of mine asked me what would happen if I was not ordained." He had my undivided attention. I was glad that he had characterized me as a friend. I also hoped that he wasn't hiding behind the pulpit to confront me. My worries were misplaced. The silence and defeat he had displayed in my office were turned to bold assurance.

> Who I am and what I do is not completed in ordination. Ordination is an act of the church, the body of Christ to be sure, but a fragile and imperfect vessel. I have responded to the call I have from God and prepared for ordination, and I hope that the church will find me fit for that ministry. But my friend's question led me to ask, What is the foundation of who I am? On what do I stand that cannot be granted or denied?

The sermon went on to speak of the unity of the body of Christ in vocation, an inheritance and a share in the ongoing work of Christ in the world. Brad assured the congregation of their baptismal vocation and its irrevocable promise, offered as God's gift without price. It is an inheritance unblemished and undefiled, on which we all could stand in assurance and trust of the abundant grace of God.

Several months later I was attending a covenant discipleship meeting that gathered members of our suburban church in *koinonia* near where they worked downtown. The focus of the group was to reflect on discipleship in the workplace, to understand faith in the context of work. Executives, corporate accountants, leaders in health care, and brokers from high-profile firms were among the members. The group was new within the year and met every other week. With tight schedules to meet, the group began and ended punctually.

Bob arrived uncharacteristically late. His impeccable wardrobe was a bit askew. When asked politely why he was late, Bob shared that the bond market had fallen apart that morning and that he was scrambling to put his portfolio back together. He had too much cash in his account and needed to get it back in circulation. I was getting a quick lesson in brokerage life. One of the equities traders voiced the dangers and how it might affect Bob's place at the firm. Hearing that, I asked him why he had come when there was so much riding on the minute-by-minute decisions. Bob replied:

> I realized midway through the morning what was going on and the pressure I was under to salvage this thing. There were some hard ethical choices I had to make, but I made them. Perhaps it will cost me my job, but it was the right thing to do. I am here because I realized that the preacher a few months ago was right. I may be a broker today, but tomorrow they can take that away from me. But I am still Bob, a baptized child of God. I can't lose that. You, gathered here as the church, remind me of that; and I need to be here.

Bob made it through that difficult day yet experienced a new sense of himself and the priorities of his life and work. The group continued to meet faithfully.

The next season Deanne came to the group with a difficult situation at work. She administered a huge staff at an important institution in the city. Major budget cuts were going to affect her personnel, forcing substantial layoffs. Deanne had always made it a practice to hire persons with physical and mental disabilities who could use their specific skills in her department. She was under pressure to retain employees who had the widest range of skills so that they could be deployed in the broadest range of jobs. It was a slick way of excluding many of those with disabilities from the pool of protected workers. Deanne came to lunch with the

80

koinonia and related her story. Another manager wondered why she was here and not planning strategy for this difficult meeting. Deanne replied:

> First, I need you to help me put on the full armor of God and encourage me to get up on the wall with the big guns. Second, and most important, I needed to come and be reminded of Bob, a baptized child of God. . . . He reminds me that I am one too. I needed to remember that.

As we have already noted in an earlier chapter, baptismal identity and vocation are key to our understanding of the purpose and relationship of mentoring. The foundation of the work of mentoring is not exclusive to the clergy. Brad powerfully testified to the truth of his empowerment for vocation as rooted in baptism. The call to baptismal identity in vocation was a powerful and transforming element in the lives of those who mentored one another in the *koinonia* that Bob and Deanne attended.

Baptismal identity is embraced as a guiding narrative as persons engage the Christian story found in Scripture and expounded in Christian history and theology. The language of Jesus' parables regarding stewardship and management grew to frame and inform the life of a broker who, at a certain point in his career, was able to let go of that identity as ultimately formative and make a transition to another field of endeavor. The freedom and courage to make those life-changing decisions emerged with a growing sense of discipleship and vocation of his life.

In order to locate the place of the mentoring role as it has been established in the United Methodist ministry preparation process, as well as its promise for pastoral ministry growing out of the baptismal relationship, it seems wise to sketch the *environment* within which this occurs. Too often the mentoring roles of candidacy and clergy mentoring are described as pieces of the process or parts of the machinery of "making clergy" or of "producing effective leaders." These mechanical terms may belie an unconscious affirmation of the contemporary notions of occupation and the fragmenting of society over against which Christian vocation stands. Thus, in this chapter, I provide a sketch of the environment of the United Methodist ministry preparation process as situated in the encompassing frame of the baptismal covenant.

It greatly concerns me that when persons present themselves for candidacy or are in the provisional process and under the care of a clergy mentor, United Methodist polity does not explicitly identify any further mentoring should such persons be discontinued. I have dealt with many people who have moved through the mentoring process of the church and have been denied (perhaps accurately and rightly) either certification as a candidate or ordination as a deacon or an elder. Without further dedicated vocational mentoring, the message to these persons is clear: Neither do you possess the gifts and skills evident for the ordained or certified ministry of the church nor is there a vocation for you outside the ordained that the church actually cares about and affirms in its official structures. The connexion breaks down, as the mentoring role is not continued either by the ministry preparation process or in connecting a person to a mentor who will give attention and blessing to the ongoing vocational discernment and commitment that is the promised inheritance of baptism. The establishment of the mentoring role for the ordination and ministry process necessitates a deeper responsibility to connect it to the baptismal covenant and mentoring in light of the vocational implications.

God, Maker and Preserver of All Things

The first principle of the creeds and articles of faith focuses on God, the maker and preserver of all things. Explicit in this first confession is an overarching interest and investment in the whole range of experience within the created order, especially in the endeavors of human beings, individual and communal.

However, despite the confession of the church, the experience of the contemporary world and often the lived practice of the church have lost the life force and implications of the overarching transcendence of God. In Jesus Christ, we confess that we have known the unifying, eschatological work to which we are called and in which we can willfully participate. Yet the experience of the church and its practice have the capacity to fragment and compartmentalize rather than to unify and heal persons toward the realization of the eschatological promise. John Taylor has framed his observations of the contemporary covenants of society.

If man shall not live by bread alone, so neither shall he live by politics alone, or by religion, or by science, or by art alone. Each is a moral community; no one of them is a sufficient community. The fragmenting claims of the domains of civilized life have by our ignorant assent become the literal terror of the world. For they have suspended the conditions of the fundamental human covenant which is beyond them all, the covenant without which at last all dignity in all men shall be cancelled in all roles—the dignity of saints and scientists as well as the dignity of marketers, and the dignity of saints and scientists no less than the dignity of marketers.[1]

Following World War II there was renewed interest in the relationship between the concept of Christian vocation and occupation in the world. More and more the world of work was seen as a human construction, with no relation to the implications of faith, except the spiritual life of a person who participates in the workplace. In the experience of most Christians, the relationship with God increasingly became a private matter. The historic spiritual and theological implications of the purpose of the human community and its endeavor in response to the revelation, or incarnation, of God were largely domesticated and personalized. With that, the church lost a corporate sense of Christian vocation beyond the institutional church and its needs. The church began to occupy a sphere related more to the domestic life and was shunned as a formative influence in the economic or political life. Many in the church saw activism as either prophetic witness "over against" the world or "meddling" in a place the church shouldn't be. In either case, the person who participated in both the church and the economic/political structures experienced a fragmented identity and loyalty.

The hedge between the spheres of church and world has strengthened dramatically among Protestants since the colonial period. Work and industry were Puritan ideas of righteousness, a utilitarian way to heaven and/or wealth. The individual quickly supplanted the sense of community; and covenant theology (in terms of community) disintegrated. This was accompanied by a particular kind of pietism that emphasized the internal life with God and turned away from the religious community's ties to vocation. By the nineteenth century, religious life in American Protestantism looked to success and an optimistic interpretation of the gospel that seemed to harmonize the service of God and Mammon as a sign of God's blessing. Spiritual experiences were refined as internal confirmations and emotional proofs of God's working in a person's life. The response to God was focused on fidelity to domestic moralities and personal, behavioral issues that bore little relationship to vocation; so two meanings of vocation gained prominence. When applied to work outside the church, *vocation* was (and for many people today remains) synonymous with *occupation* or *profession*. Within the church, vocation became the exclusive property of the *ordained.*

The Social Gospel movement of the late nineteenth and early twentieth centuries attempted to overturn the sanctification of the search for wealth and emphasized Christians' social responsibilities. However, this effort failed to reestablish a unifying vision of God's work in the world, and Christian vocation in the broadest sense, as an instrument of healing and redemption. The Protestant vocational ethic that had responded to the first principle of faith—"diligence plus thrift equals service to God"— had been replaced by an ethic expressed as "diligence plus thrift equals success." The focus had shifted from vocation as related to the work of God to vocation as human occupation and the production of material things. In this construction, a human being became part of the science and mechanism of production itself. The Puritan notion of efficiency had shifted from a human experience to a mechanical one.

> With the industrial Revolution the ancient myth of the Occident—a historical, eschatological myth of hope—has been fragmented, bifurcating and spatializing the inner and outer worlds. On the outer (institutional) side the fragment concentrates its effort on utilitarian goals, eventually promoting bureaucratization and the concentration of corporate power economic and political, thus imprisoning the human being in a cage. . . . This myth of "progress," a descendant of earlier dreams of the millennium, has been accompanied and supported by the myths of positivism and scientism, antimetaphysical myths cut off from the transcendent. On the inner side, "religion" becomes a fragment; instead of maintaining the prophetic wholeness of its initial eschatological and institutional thrust, it retreats to the realm of a spurious and uncreative privatization. Separated from each other (that is, spatialized), both the inner and the outer fragment become demonic, with the consequence that neither of them fructifies or corrects the other.[2]

The role of the Christian mentor within the economy of the church and its ministry stands over against a fragmented sense of vocation, *praxis,* or practice. For mentoring to have any integrity beyond a screening mechanism for a specific profession in the church, it must take seriously the renewal of a holistic and inclusive view of Christian vocation that emerges out of the understanding of God as the maker and preserver of all things. The vocational aspect of the first principle is enhanced in the Statement of Faith of the Korean Methodist Church and in the Modern Affirmation, as found in *The United Methodist Hymnal.*

> We believe in the reign of God
>> as the divine will realized in human society,
>> and in the family of God,
>> where we are all brothers and sisters.
>>> (Korean Methodist Church)
>
> * * *
>
> We believe in God the Father,
>> infinite in wisdom, power, and love,
>> whose mercy is over all his works,
>> and whose will is ever directed to his children's good.
>>> (Modern Affirmation)[3]

Baptism is a particular expression of incorporation into the vocation of God and the body of Christ. The World Council of Churches' study *Baptism, Eucharist and Ministry* spends a great deal of attention on the wholeness of life promised and expressed in baptism. A person is divinely called through baptism to be part of God's mighty acts of salvation in the world. The vocation in which God calls us is a divine means to redeem the fallenness of creation and community through the ongoing work of the body of Christ. To become part of the divine vocation through baptism is to move toward healing the fragmentation, brokenness, and sin of personal and communal life and life in the world in order to realize God's purposes. In this sense, vocation gives purpose for life beyond fulfillment of the self, beyond the community, and beyond the mechanisms of the world; yet it invests all of the spheres of life with transcendent purpose and meaning.

Baptism promises a share in Christ's vocation in the world, moving a person beyond an understanding of work as either exhaustingly mechanical (thus being able to be *burned out*) or as simply temporal and temporarily utilitarian. It was this aspect of baptismal identity that Bob and Deanne sought out so they would not be consumed by the overwhelming reality of temporary utility, and so they could clothe themselves in the transcendent vocation of Christ of which they were a part.

The call of God in Scripture in the Hebrew Bible is to be part of the people of Israel and, in the New Testament, to be part of the Way and later the body of Christ. In addition to this general call are particular callings and gifts given to fulfill the needs of the community; but all these gifts were understood as part of the economy of God. The story of God revealed in Scripture and incarnated in Christ gives coherent meaning and form to our lives. The word for the gathering of community—*ekklesia*—was co-opted from the Greek meaning "called out to gather." It named the church as distinct from the economy of the world, as if in a separate sphere. However, we should recall that the gathering of the *ekklesia* is also leaven for life and work in the world, redeeming and inviting participation in divine vocation.

The importance of the narrative of Scripture and the historic tradition of the church is crucial to forming and reforming the frame, content, hope, and virtue of a person's life and purpose. People find themselves in the story and become part of it. It defines and forms the *praxis*, passions, and eschatological hope toward which a person and community move.[4]

Connected by Vocation

Cam sat in the back pew, with his wife and a friend. Like his friend, Cam was an engineer—a civil engineer, to be exact. He spent much of his life designing and engineering the Massachusetts Turnpike and other public works projects in the Boston area. I was convinced that leaving the back of the bulletin blank was meant not only for children to draw on during the sermon but also for engineers to draw schematics on. I wasn't ever clear that I had reached either of them with my sermons; and they were too polite to say. As I was moving through an Advent sermon on John the Baptist's quoting of Isaiah, "The voice of one crying out in the wilderness: 'Prepare the way of the Lord, make his paths straight'" (Matt. 3:3), I looked at Cam and it came to me that John was calling the civil engineers to be the first employed for the reign of God. I quickly moved the sermon in that direction. Cam's attention was riveted on the pulpit.

On the way out of the service, it was clear that Cam had been moved. Small puddles of tears gathered in his eyes. He liked the sermon and he knew why. I had no idea what transpired inside him. All I was trying to do was get his attention. He was thankful that I pointed out the importance of the civil engineers to the work of God. It was when the Hoover Dam project was being completed, he said, that he first got the sense that his life would be devoted to civil engineering. He was moved to dedicate his life to making the world a better place for people to live and to forming their communities. He felt that it was much like the callings pastors talked about. He once shared with a pastor his call to be a civil engineer and not a clergyperson. The pastor expressed little interest in following up on the conversation. Cam became a civil engineer anyway.

Over the months following the sermon, Cam and I met over coffee to talk about his call and his sense of vocation. It was an understanding of purpose and virtue that he had tried to sustain on his own for some time. But as time went along, the sense of "calling" waned; and he got caught up in the routine of the job, in the politics and battles over funding and influencing the movers and shakers, and in the infighting that plagues public projects. Civil engineering had become "a job" for Cam. That was, until he heard the story of John the Baptist recast as a call to civil engineers to build the highway of God. Cam cherished the moment when he could retrieve the extended version of the passage from memory. "Didn't it go, 'Prepare a highway for our God. Every valley shall be exalted, every mountain and hill made low, the crooked places made straight and the rough places made a plain'? Beautiful verse for the Christmas music, but you helped me put it together as the work of my life. That is what I do! You helped me touch my calling again and the reason I got into this in the first place."

In talking with Cam, it came clear to me that the first calling and vocational commissioning in the gospel was not for someone to become an ordained member of the clergy or even a disciple. It was John's call to the vocation of civil engineer to prepare the highway of Christ. This connexion to his call helped Cam revitalize his commitment to his work and the purpose for it. He shared his faith connexion with a younger member of his team, who was a Coptic Christian. They shared their faith together—and as different in worship practice as a Copt and a United Methodist are, they held a common vocation and grew in what that might mean in daily practice. Cam helped me understand the importance of roads in human society and in the building of community. "As an heir of Wesley's circuit riders, as a Methodist preacher you should know that!" Cam exclaimed. "Where would we be without roads? Probably Methodist circuit walkers!"

Cam grew up in a church culture that had relegated vocation to the calling of the clergy. The apostle Paul faced similar divisions in Greek culture. Aristotle insisted that it was demoralizing and degrading to work with one's hands. Cicero felt that free men who took up a trade were doing something humiliating because it was beneath freedom.[5] Furthermore, artisans were considered incapable of the higher forms of civic duty. They could not devote themselves to helping the neighbor, the civic life, or their own soul. Therefore, they were incapable of achieving virtue. Paul contended with these attitudes in his epistolary correspondence. In a direct confrontation of the social disassociation between virtue and work, Paul identified himself as a tentmaker. Yet he modeled the development of the soul, the love of neighbor, and the availability of the truth of philosophy and theology rooted in Christ as available to all: slave, free, Jew, Greek, male and female. The tentmaker's shop floor was as much the place of *praxis* as the synagogue or Areopagus.

Vocation is determined inwardly at the point where God's willing and working is united with humanity's will and work (Phil. 2:12–13). Vocation includes the discerning of personal gifts and graces, given by God, for vocational purposes in the world. Paul encourages us to move from a sense of the precariousness of human experience to a clear and robust confidence that emerges from participating in the vocation of God—a journey that liberates us from the "goal-oriented" impulses generated in the corruption of vocation as self-interest and self-fulfillment. Paul places Christian vocation as participation in the arc of human experience between distinctive memory and distinctive hope, between Christ's first coming and Christ's final coming. Or, if we want to broaden the scope to include those who "know not Christ," in order to empower vocation in the *ekklesia* of the world, we could say vocation exists between creation and fulfillment.[6]

The Priesthood of All Believers

"The Order for Consecration and Ordinations: A Recognition of Our Common Ministry" in *The United Methodist Book of Worship* establishes the calling and vocation of the ordained in the context of the vocation of each Christian as a member of the priesthood of all believers. In so doing, The United Methodist Church continues to affirm in its baptismal theology and ecclesiology the focus of the Protestant Reformation. As United Methodists meet at annual conference, the bishop gathers the church and reminds them of their identity and inheritance.

> Ministry is the work of God,
>> done by the people of God
>> and given to each Christian as vocation.
> Through baptism
>> all Christians are made part of the priesthood of all believers,
>> the church made visible in the world.
> God in Christ through the Holy Spirit
>> empowers us to live as witnesses of God's grace and love.
> We are to bear witness in and through the life of the Church
>> and to be faithful in our daily lives.

> Therefore, in celebration of our common ministry,
>> I call upon all God's people gathered here:
> Remember your baptism and be thankful.[7]

In a revision of the services for the ordering of ministry in The United Methodist Church, the theological foundations continue to anchor the ordained ministry within the general ministry, calling, and vocation of all baptized Christians. In ordination, the Holy Spirit acts to maintain the priority of the gospel by setting apart men and women called to apostolic leadership.

The pattern for this response to the call is provided in the development of the early church. The apostles led in prayer, teaching and preaching, ordered the spiritual and temporal life of the community, established leadership for the ministry of service, and provided for the proclamation of the gospel to new persons and in new places. The early church, through the laying on of hands, set apart persons with

89

responsibility to preach, to teach, to administer the sacraments, to nurture, to heal, to gather the community in worship, and to send them forth in witness. The church also set apart other persons to care for the physical needs of others, reflecting the concerns for the people of the world. . . .

Ordination to this ministry is a gift from God to the church. In ordination, the church affirms and continues the apostolic ministry through persons empowered by the Holy Spirit. . . .

Ministry in the Christian church is derived from the ministry of Christ, who calls all persons to receive God's gift of salvation and follow in the way of love and service. The whole church receives and accepts this call, and all Christians participate in this continuing ministry.[8]

The text *Services for the Ordering of Ministry in The United Methodist Church* continues:

Acts of ordination and commissioning, as well as consecration and certifying, are anchored in the sacrament of baptism and the ministry of the baptized. These sign-acts [ordination and commissioning] are based on what is already implicit in baptism, and rest upon the essential ministry given to all Christians in baptism. . . . Anchored in the baptismal call to lives of love, justice, and service, there are some Christians whose "gifts, evidence of God's grace, and promise of future usefulness are affirmed by the community, and who respond to God's call by offering themselves in leadership as ordained ministers."[9]

Martin Luther

The enduring identity of the church as the priesthood of all believers has been a formative gift from Martin Luther's reformation of the church in the sixteenth century. Luther confronted an ecclesiastical structure that fixed a great divide between the clergy and the laity. The calling of the clergy was to enter a "spiritual estate" above that of the "temporal estate" of the laity. A "calling" or "vocation" was understood as to the "divine order," and ordination was the sacrament of transportation between one and the other. Any contemporary vestige of the separation of the clergy from the laity in such an impermeable way may hearken to this understanding of the spiritual exclusivity of the clergy.

Luther sharpened his attack on the viability of this structure as truly Christian and affirmed the common ministry and priesthood of all believers in his treatise *The Christian Nobility*. In it he returned the authorization for Christian vocation as issuing from baptism. Each Christian had his or her own work to do as part of the vocation of Christ. Ordination was not a special status before God but rather the delegation of responsibilities by the congregation to one who had gifts to organize and look out for the interests of the rest. However, this did not give such a person a different status before God. Each believer held his or her status as an inheritance granted in baptism through Christ, as a child of God.[10]

Although Luther was able to challenge and collapse the separate estates into the common ministry of the priesthood of all believers, his view of the broader community was fixed in established spheres and stations of work and influence. Although persons were baptized into the common ministry of the church, they came to their occupations and professions in the traditional means of assuming their lot in life. Luther's notion of the vocation of Christ in the world focused on faith expressed in the love of neighbor. The critical aspect for Luther was that believers be aware that the mission of a Christian in the various contexts of life and in their concrete tasks was the love of God. Responding to the call of Christ in vocation was a means of self-emptying in the love of God that held the scriptural promise of the presence of Christ in all.

In the comprehensive structure of his reforming theology, Luther places vocation between baptism and the final resurrection. For him, there are two realms (heaven and earth), two contending powers (God and the devil), and two antagonistic powers within the self (old and new). Human beings live in the earthly realm but yearn for the heavenly (which will be revealed fully after death or in the final resurrection); are under the law of sin but liberated from the law by faith in the gospel; are dying to the old in the daily death of Christ and raised to the new in the promise of resurrection; and are tempted by the devil and forced to choose sides in the great struggle to serve God's creative power.[11]

The vision of the two realms is a helpful frame for understanding the world as moving toward the heavenly as the inheritance and work of a Christian. The call for relaxing the distinctions between the things of God and the things of Mammon and the attempt to harmonize them, considered earlier in the chapter, chimes with the attempt to relax the tension between the two realms. From this perspective, it is possible to trace the dimming of the community's awareness of the dynamic divine force necessary for moving the human journey in the direction of heaven in the course of daily living. Luther was clear that we live in a fallen world and participate in it. However, in the context of the world, the Christian is freed from the law by dying and rising with Christ each day. The question of faith raised for the Christian every day has to do with what God commanded, learning the will of God, and looking out for the neighbor's need. In this way a person is freed from self-centered concerns, which require the control of law, and is able to attend and respond to the gospel and the heavenly direction of vocation.

Meanwhile, the strict social order and stations of life in which Luther's ideas of vocation were framed had begun to collapse. Trade was expanding, along with the accompanying influence of financiers and bankers who controlled credit, capital, and trade. In Italy and Flanders, owners exploited labor for their own ends. In Spain and Portugal, the influence of the church was torn between the financial needs of colonization and the mission of the church. Luther's reaction was to yearn for the more stable and stratified society in which the gospel operated on a static rather than a chaotic world. He was not interested in the engagement of what was emerging.[12]

John Calvin

The impact of Luther's concept of Christian vocation gained broader authority and greater exposure when John Calvin adopted and adapted it to his social theology and theory. He linked Luther's religious motifs directly to sociopolitical concerns not wedded or deferential to the established structures of society. Calvin's influence was more expansive than Luther's and more ecumenical in scope, bringing revolution to social structure through active, radical force that sought to penetrate all spheres, public and private, with the influence of the gospel. The impact of the presence of the gospel and the influence of the church in renovating social, political, and economic structures can be observed in

Calvin's Geneva, Knox's Scotland, Cromwell's England, and the Puritans' New England. While these lasting accomplishments have been secularized and cut from their Christian roots, a residue is still present in these societies.

Luther developed his theology of vocation within a framework of a "natural" stratification of society (not monied or commercial but small-town shops and peasant subsistence). Calvin's world, on the other hand, was entrepreneurial, urban, and international. He reflected the apostle Paul's need to translate the gospel from its Semitic, agrarian roots to the urban networks of the wider world. Within the swirl of activity embraced by the Calvinist social vision, the spontaneity of God's bestowal of gifts and the calling of love were less important than they had been in Luther. Instead, they were replaced with a quest for the proper ordering of life, individual and corporate, to respond to the complexity that had been unleashed. Calvin was concerned that life, in its complexity, must be ordered in such a fashion that it would not be thrown into chaos. God is honored to the extent that this societal ordering is effective.

Calvin was convinced that Christians could not withdraw from the world or be isolated from it just because it was chaotic and often horrifying. The individual's and the church's vocation was to oppose the sin and deprivation of the world and to overcome and subdue it to the good order of God. The instruments of the world were to be utilized for godly ends.[13] Similar to Luther, for Calvin, the general calling of a Christian in the world was to do justice and mercy as an expression of the love of God. Yet, the particular calling of a person was less experiential and more to a specific occupation and daily work as contributing to the right and goodly order.

Growing out of the social vision of the Reformers was the need for voluntary organizations to establish goodly order. These forums were gathered for give-and-take discussions for the purpose of examining the status quo and subjecting it to criticism in order to change it. To participate in these structures, it was crucial that persons had the appropriate spiritual disposition. People characterized by prudence, serious and sober self-discipline, and educational attainment found social contract with one another and organized into committees; rules of law were created and constitutional organs brought into being—all to serve as agents of social ordering and instruments of change. In this process, Calvin's ethics became intensified and externalized, as participation in the process became more accessible to the average person through the emerging social forms.

However, it is imperative to remember that the Christian disciplines of formation and the focus on the gospel and the glory of God became separated from the economic and political forms to which they gave birth. Earlier in the chapter, I showed how the discipline of faith was replaced by an accommodation of the ways of God to the ways of Mammon. Similarly here, the structures of participation birthed by Calvin's understanding of Christian vocation were separated from the gospel. It must always be in the forefront of our thinking that the glory of God is the sole purpose for the vocation of a Christian, whether in worship or work, in study or prayer.[14]

This is a critical point in establishing mentoring roles within the church. Designed to mentor a person into vocation as it emerges in baptismal calling, these roles *must* keep the focus on the grace and glory of God at the heart of the relationship. Just as it was possible for any of the social structures, personal enfranchisement, or governing rules that emerged from the vocational vitality of the Reformation to continue in ignorance of their birth in providence, so too it is possible for the mentoring structures of the church to forget their divine origin. Therefore, the mentor must be a reminder, a sign, and a representative presence of God's gracious call and claim in the life of one seeking to respond to God's act of grace. The mentor is also a reminder to the community of colleagues and the church as a whole that the vocation we discern is Christ's. Vocation is always for the glory of God.

A Congregation Embraces Vocation and Organizes Mentoring *Koinonia*

During my pastoral ministry, I have found a yearning readiness in churches to engage the workaday world with the gospel faith. Yet laity have voiced great frustration over the church's seeming preoccupation with keeping its own institutional machinery going and attending to the church's "business" rather than focusing its time and efforts on the church's *true* business: to empower people to be Christ's disciples in the world and to carry the message of the faith into their daily experience. The result of the church's inattention to the importance of baptismal vocation is that very often persons who have awakened to vocation believe that ordained ministry is the only option for living out their vocation. My experience as a pastor over many years in a variety of settings has convinced me that United Methodists will have a more empowered church, more effective clergy, and a more vital ministry by the whole people of God if we renew the Reformers' invitation to vocation and make our church's baptismal and ordination liturgies our daily focus and attention.

In an effort to understand how a local church might be effective in this endeavor, twenty-four persons participated in a survey and in a reflection group around the relationship between their religion and their economic life. The goal was to get a clearer focus on how participants viewed the importance of their faith for their work.

Nineteen of the participants understood their work to be a direct extension of their Christian commitment. They included a homemaker, a teacher, a machinist, a bookseller, a jeweler, a real estate agent, a business manager, a newspaper manager, a corporate daycare director, an electronics engineer, a computer firm consultant, librarians, secretaries, nurses, salespeople, and managers. Only the check packer and the purchasing agent (and later, a nurse) did not find any connexion. The corporate accountant struggled with the issue but was beginning to see the connexions between the biblical notions of stewardship and his occupation. When the results were revealed in the first meeting following the survey, the purchasing agent began to interact with the accountant, started making some of those connexions, and began to see the implications for his job.

One of the nurses and the homemaker found that their Christian calling was carried out in the very nature of their occupations. Interestingly, the nurse who made this connexion felt that the church should be directly involved with the hospital to give ethical resources in its decision-making processes. The second of the two nurses, who did not make the connexion between her Christian commitment and the nature of her occupation, felt that the church had no business dealing with the direction or policies of the hospital.

Twenty-one of the members felt that if their occupation were an extension of their Christian commitment, it was because of what they brought to it. Overwhelmingly, participants felt that it was in person-to-person relationships that faith affects occupation most critically. They mentioned several personal attributes through which their faith gets lived out in these relationships:

being helpful to others; honesty; conversations that reflect respect for values rather than conversations exhibiting crude language; lifestyle modeling; compassion; caring; and tolerance. Another attribute the group sought to express more effectively was the ability to invite others to church, either to worship or to participate in other activities. Specifically, they wanted to be able to introduce those with whom they worked to Jesus Christ without being obnoxious or judgmental. "I want to be able to introduce them to the Jesus I know, without all the rhetoric and other demands I see advocated or modeled by some television evangelists or those in the office who are derisively called 'Christian' because they never give 'it' a rest."

Seventy-five percent of the group felt that their faith had no effect on the development of policy in the workplace. The larger the business in which people worked, the more remote this possibility seemed. The exceptions were proprietors of small businesses. Said the jeweler, "I am a Christian. I am the boss. I set the policy!" The bookseller found that his policies were Christian because his prices did not exploit either seller or buyer. For the machinist, who did some supervision on the shop floor, part of his supervisory responsibility was to scrutinize policies for fairness; and he was often called upon to render judgments in terms of employee performance or behavior. He found his religious training to be helpful but wished it were more current. He often found it difficult to connect his faith to the situation in which he found himself. Many times he did have some idea of the biblical or moral principle he was using in dealing with a particular issue. However, he admitted that, more often than not, it was based on a hunch; and that made him uncomfortable and unsure. He noted that more direct discussion and reflection on issues in the workplace would be of immense help.

As many of the issues arising from the survey results were reported, the group wanted to stop and discuss the issues and offer insights. One of the more adventuresome and outspoken members of the group made a profound statement about the survey process, the evening's discussion, and his perceptions of the church's role in the current situation. I paraphrase his words here:

> The sustained conversation that I have after church with a group of six or seven friends at coffee hour is where the real progress is made, for me, in understanding what I am supposed to do. Your sermon may provoke

an idea or challenge me to think about something, but it is the discussion that is most helpful to me. But the efforts are halting at best. There is always the tug to mingle, socialize, and get to know the rest of the church. Disciplined reflection, biblical study, and intentional gatherings for spiritual formation with a sustained group of people would be helpful. Perhaps the church needs to do this with laity more directly. . . . And I think that the church needs to do some counseling to help us with our faith walk and our vocation, either in choosing a career that will be part of our faith walk or in dealing with issues on the job.

Another member of the group carried the thought forward.

Whenever I have thought about Christian vocation, it was always in terms of the clergy. When I was growing up, I always went to church. I spoke up in Sunday school and even spoke in the church when I was in junior high school. My minister and some of the older members of the church kept saying to me over and over again that I should be a minister. I didn't want to be a minister. I had other interests that I thought I was good at. When I told my minister that, he seemed to lose interest in my future. I have seen it too often: The only vocational interest promoted in the church with any sense of blessing and worth is to become a member of the clergy. Like none of the rest of us does anything important to the church, unless we serve on a committee or perhaps become a member of the lay staff. I think that the church must help its members discern their vocation, not as a career counselor or job referrals but to help make the connections in terms of what we might be able to do in the world. I want to know how Jesus is with me in what I do, or that I am with him. And I don't mean to throw this all on the pastor. Groups like this, talking about their job, helping one another, being free to be Christians with helping one another, but talk about what's going on in our businesses. When I go to the "reunion group," we talk about spiritual matters and how they get lived out in the family and we may get to talk about work. But not enough.

I spoke to the group about Wesley's class meetings, and we discussed the idea. Within the next few months, several small groups began to meet informally. One of the most consistent groups met on Sunday morning during adult Sunday school. This group helped one of its members move through a roller-coaster ride of job layoffs, reduced work hours, and the restructuring of his spouse's company that kept her in the dark for months on end. During a time when all manner of self-doubt and insecurity about the future were plaguing this group member, he was being supported in his role as the congregation's lay leader. It encouraged him to hear members repeating to him the help and support he had given them over the years. Moreover, he became an inspiration and spiritual support to many of his coworkers in getting through the difficult days that confronted the company. At the same time, a chemist at a large research facility was exploring his spiritual life in a deep, broad, and intentionally experimental way. He had reached a point in his life when he concluded that the promises of reward held out by his profession and workplace were woefully inadequate to fill his soul and sustain him spiritually. The group listened, reflected with him, questioned honestly and lovingly when they felt that he had gone astray, and walked with him. They wanted to know how he might bring what he was learning in the group into his lab. "Well," he said, "I guess I am old enough and perceived as wise enough to lead by example. I do my work and I do it well; they respect that. But I also want them to see that obsession with work and reports and all of that stuff is not all there is to life. I want them to know that there is also beauty, and suffering is real, and there is a heart to life that keeps beating. And God (or whoever it is that put this all together and watches us or touches us) blesses it all!"

The role of the faith community, the focus of *koinonia,* and the particular attention of the Christian mentor help discern and articulate the call so that it can be voiced and understood in a comprehensive manner. Reflecting on the substance of the call and the invited response are key. Encouraging and empowering specific steps as responsive witness to what God has done in the grace of calling are imperative aspects of the accompanying partner's work. Further, the community's prophetic task to shape a call—recalling the origin (God), the context (the covenant of vocation), the direction (God's promises, which culminate in the *eschaton*), and the attitude of response (knowing that God's call is not a matter indifferent to God and therefore requires a humble response)—is crucial to its response through mentors, *koinonia,* and the ethos of the general vocation of the people of God.

These areas form the touchstones of the mentoring relationship— call, covenant, context, credo, and connexion. While they guide mentors in a particular way, these touchstones are the essential areas of the journey of all Christians in vocation.

Notes

1. John F. A. Taylor, *The Masks of Society: An Inquiry into the Covenants of Civilization* (New York: Appleton-Century-Crofts, 1966), 125.

2. James Luther Adams, "The Phenomenology of Fragmentation and the Ecology of Dreams," in *The Prophethood of All Believers*, edited and with an introduction by George K. Beach (Boston: Beacon, 1986), 228–29.

3. "A Statement of Faith of the Korean Methodist Church" and "A Modern Affirmation," *The United Methodist Hymnal* (Nashville: The United Methodist Publishing House, 1989), 884, 885.

4. James W. Fowler, *Becoming Adult, Becoming Christian* (San Francisco: Harper and Row, 1984), surveys the importance of narrative in Christian vocation. He enjoins the work of Alasdair MacIntyre, *After Virtue* (Notre Dame, Indiana: University of Notre Dame Press, 1981), and David Tracy, *The Analogical Imagination: Christian Theology and the Culture of Pluralism* (New York: Crossroad, 1981), to explore the importance of narrative in the formation of vocation.

5. Ronald F. Hock, *The Social Context of Paul's Ministry: Tentmaking and Apostleship* (Philadelphia: Fortress, 1980), 36.

6. Paul S. Minear, *To Die and to Live: Christ's Resurrection and Christian Vocation* (New York: Seabury, 1977), 40*ff*, and William A. Beardslee, *Human Achievement and Divine Vocation in the Message of Paul* (Naperville, IL: Alec R. Allensen, Inc., 1961), 11.

7. *The United Methodist Book of Worship* (Nashville: The United Methodist Publishing House, 1992), 686.

8. *The Book of Discipline of The United Methodist Church—2008* (Nashville: The United Methodist Publishing House, 2008), paragraphs 302, 303.1, 301.1; see also paragraphs 120–138. Used by permission.

9. *Services for the Ordering of Ministry in The United Methodist Church*, 208 (Prepared by the General Board of Discipleship, the General Board of Higher Education and Ministry, and the General Commission of Christian Unity and Interreligious Concerns, in collaboration with The Council of Bishops. Approved by the 2008 General Conference), 8. Available online at http://www.gbod.org/worship. See also *Book of Discipline*, paragraph 301.2.

10. Martin Luther, "To the Christian Nobility of the German Nation Concerning the Reform of the Christian Estate," in *Luther's Works*, trans. Charles M. Jacobs and James Atkinson; ed. Jaroslav Pelikan and Helmut T. Lehmann (Philadelphia: Fortress, 1966), 44:123–30. Several recent studies that expand upon the Christian heritage indicate a renewed interest in the importance of vocation. I commend two here: Douglas J. Schuurman, *Vocation: Discerning Our Callings in Life* (Grand Rapids: Eerdmans, 2004), and Gary D. Badcock, *The Way of Life: A Theology of Christian Vocation* (Grand Rapids: Eerdmans, 1998).

11. See Gustaf Wingren, *Luther on Vocation* (Philadelphia: Muhlenberg Press, 1957), 163*ff.* "The law is a fixed requirement of conduct, thus bondage. The divine command is creatively new, breaks through the law to meet life. The command to love your neighbor cannot be learned in advance, but depends on the neighbor." Learning to die to one's own interests and daily rising to hear and learn (in the experience of life) God's command helps to discharge one's vocation.

12. R. H. Tawney, *Religion and the Rise of Capitalism: A Historical Study* (New York: Harcourt, Brace, and Company, 1926), 89.

13. Ernst Troeltsch, *The Social Teachings of the Christian Churches* (London: George Allen & Unwin Ltd., 1931), 604.

14. Ibid.

Chapter 4

THE TOUCHSTONES

The scriptural narrative provides us with vibrant examples of the crucial elements of a life of faith. In preaching through the three-year lectionary cycle a dozen times in the context of the congregations I pastored, I realized that I was mentoring many of them in their Christian vocation from the pulpit, in Bible study, during pastoral visits, and in formal sessions designed specifically for the task of mentoring. For a handy pneumonic device, I speak of the five "C"s of mentoring: Call, Covenant, Context, Credo, and Connexion. These are the five touchstones of mentoring.

The patterns are not always the same in terms of order, but the touchstones emerge in a variety of ways through the mentoring journey. Wander with me for a moment through your favorite scriptural passages about God's call in a person's life—from the story of Ruth to Paul's dramatic Damascus Road experience. In the course of each of these biblical stories (and there are many), the purpose and direction of the person's life is shaped by God's *call*, either through direct encounter with God in which God provides direction or by a growing awareness through the witness of another person or the community. A promise is made that articulates the relationship and what is given and received from each in the form of a *covenant*. Many times the covenant involves the changing of someone's name or identity. At other times, the covenant requires of the person a new way of being or a new understanding of identity and of the purpose of what he or she does. God's call and the covenant into which we enter are not mere affirmations of the status quo; rather, they form the basis of a commission, a "sending" into a particular *context* to live into and fulfill the covenant. Words such as *rise up, go, follow, hurry, journey,* and *come to* are often associated with the commissioning to context.

These three elements form a powerful hermeneutic that develops a person's sense of self in relationship to God and vocation; but they do not do so in a linear fashion. Instead, the three work in an interrelated way, as a cross-pollination of awareness, identity, and relationship. A stirring moment in the biblical stories and in the lives of Christians over the millennia is when their experience finds expression in a *credo*—an articulation of faith and belief in God's very being and saving activity in the world. In Christian terms, it is an illumination of the truth of Christ and the gracious work of the Holy Spirit. Luther's "Here I Stand!"; Miriam's "Song of Deliverance" on the shores of the Red Sea; Paul's testimony throughout his epistles that still frames the credo of the whole church; the Apostles' Creed; Charles Wesley's articulation of the Methodist experience in "Love's Divine"; Mary's Magnificat—all form and shape the faith that calls us and commissions us for a purpose within the encompassing, eternal purposes of God. Within the Christian tradition are creedal statements that have been adopted as authoritative and formative. Cherished theologians and pastoral leaders have written and spoken in an effort to illuminate an understanding of the ways of God that are systematic and comprehensive. These statements surround and inform the formulation of *credo*. However, let us never forget that *credo* is not a matter merely of preference or similarity to another's theology but of the witness to God of one's life.

The final touchstone is *connexion*. As I mentioned in the introduction, my use of Wesley's spelling of the term rather than the usual "connection" is deliberate. The *x* reminds us of the intersection of our own personal journey with that of the church in an inextricable manner. One cross branch without the other in the construction of the letter would leave the structure to fall, the letter without meaning, and the word without significance. Connexion indicates the accountability our life in vocation and discipleship has to the whole body of the church. Structures of expectation and accountability anchor, empower, shape, and sometimes curtail and frustrate the other aspects of the vocational journey. This is especially true in a culture that values autonomy, individual initiative, and personal achievement. The value of connexion is fundamental to the life of the church and is not a new means of empowerment. Neither does it create tension.

I think of the apostle Paul and his experience of connexion. The Jerusalem Council, the leadership of the churches of Asia Minor, the self-understandings of the gatherings in Rome—all had separate identities and means of accountability. Yet they all were crucial points of connexion for Paul. And each led to frustration and sometimes refinement in Paul's understanding of his call and his contextual covenant, as well as in the way he expressed *credo*. Whether part of the mentoring structures of the ministry preparation process or of mentoring in other partnerships, the mentor is a sign and presence of the larger connexion of the church.

Together, the touchstones form the themes and elements of the narrative that the mentor and mentee share. They focus and vitalize the authentic and genuine navigation of the partnership's paths and purposes and maintain focus on the author of the journey—God—and the intended end, namely, to give glory to God by fulfilling the vocation to which we are called and by using the gifts God has given.

It would be a great gift if persons entering into mentoring relationships could watch a skilled mentor at work to observe how he or she develops the relationship. When I ask mentors of long standing how they take the initial steps in a mentoring relationship, a common response is "Everyone is different." This may seem a bit facile and dismissive; but it testifies to the unique gifts a mentor brings, which then are married to the unique story and way of knowing and journeying brought by a mentee. It is indeed similar to wedding vows. The only ones who truly know what those simple vows mean in their lives are the two individuals who are saying them at that time. No manual or road map for the married life exists; there are only signposts and companionship.

It is important for a mentor to assemble his or her own cloud of witnesses and counselors for the mentoring task. I would love to have a transcript of the relationship of Moses and Joshua that culminated in Moses' words of commissioning: "Be strong and bold, for you are the one who will

go with this people into the land that the LORD has sworn to their ancestors to give them; and you will put them in possession of it. It is the LORD
who goes before you. He will be with you; he will not fail you or forsake
you. Do not fear or be dismayed" (Deut. 31:7–8). Or the extensive conversations and exploits Elisha and Elijah shared, from the clarification of call
and the sense of election Elisha felt when Elijah threw his mantle over him
(1 Kings 19:16–21) to the passing of that mantle with Elisha receiving the
double share of Elijah's spirit (2 Kings 2:9-14). In both cases, the blessing
of the mentor grew out of a deep sense of trust in the mentee to fulfill a
vocation and covenant that were greater than their own. It stemmed also
from a deep sense of the mentor's own call, covenant, and mission that were
quickened again in this particular relationship. It is in conceiving of the
sharing of autobiography in the light of the biography of God and God's
people that we understand the substance of the conversations.

The early mystics and spiritual writers who explored the spiritual
journey of the church wrote about their own practices of guiding and
mentoring others, articulated in relationship to Scripture and the saints of
the church. The tradition continued to the exemplary traditions of the
sixteenth and seventeenth centuries under the influence of Teresa of Avila
and Ignatius of Loyola, especially the much-adapted *Spiritual Exercises*.
The continuing renewal of the church was undergirded by the spiritual
direction given to both laity and clergy. Journals from Methodist class
meetings, Presbyterian zone meetings, Quaker meetings, and other mutual
mentoring engagements reveal the content of these engagements and
their development. Dietrich Bonhoeffer's writings and letters also give a
sense of how "life together" was focused and conducted.

In addition to the methods and examples enjoying a renewal in the
study and practice of spiritual direction are a variety of other pastoral disciplines that are gifts to the mentoring process. Although mentoring is
not a therapeutic relationship, the general wisdom of counseling and its
understanding of the human psyche and its development can be a great
resource in mentoring. Those who have had training in adult learning
models will be able to draw on the various avenues and techniques of
teaching and learning to develop and explore vocational knowledge and
understanding. There is growing interest in the skills of appreciative
inquiry and neurolinguistic programming to unlock the core passions,

commitments, interests, and meaning in the language and expression of another. There are also several strength-finders and personality indicators that have been adapted for use in the church. All of these have their place and are resources for use in the mentoring process. My review of the touchstones is not meant either to add to or to detract from this variety of arrows in the interpersonal quiver (used, hopefully, accurately to penetrate the heart and soul as an agent of the work of the Holy Spirit). Mentors bring with them the gifts and interests of a wide range of pastoral disciplines. I hope that these can be sifted together as part of the mentor's giftedness to the mentee as they journey together into vocation.

Call

To introduce the importance of call at workshops on clergy mentoring I conducted in South Africa, I began with two spirituals from the African-American tradition. They were unknown to the participants; but the melody, and then the harmonies, grew and developed as the singing went on. There was a deep resonance with the African-American remembrance of slavery and the importance of God's knowledge, care, and call in terms of identity and the Holy Spirit's empowerment to "do something" in the name of and in companionship with the Lord Jesus. Apartheid had carved a similar scar to slavery's, and the spiritual was a recognizable balm and praise for Christ's liberating grace and vocation.

> Hush. Hush. Somebody's callin' mah name.
> Hush. Hush. Somebody's callin' mah name.
> Hush. Hush. Somebody's callin' mah name.
> Oh mah Lawd, Oh mah Lawdie, what shall I do?
>
> * * *
>
> Steal away, steal away, steal away to Jesus!
> Steal away, steal away home, I ain't got long to stay here!
> My Lord calls me, He calls me by the thunder;
> The trumpet sounds with-in-a my soul,
> I ain't got long to stay here.[1]

At a break in the workshop, one of the women shared with me the reason these songs meant so much even if they had never sung them before. "Steal away" was the term that women from the coast of the Indian Ocean used when they would go west to the Drakensberg mountains and sing into the distance for their husbands and sons who had been taken to work in the gold mines of Johannesburg. The songs were also prayers, hoping that the men in the mines, in the dark bowels of the earth, would be reached and remembered—would know that "somebody's callin' mah name."

The experience of calling may be faint as in an echo of a hymn or as in a prayer carried on the wind across the savanna to the funnel of a mineshaft. It may be a vague feeling; a nudge; or a sense of rightness, direction, or fulfillment. Calling may be a clarity of purpose in oneself or a joining of oneself to a greater purpose in the world. Calling may come as a clarifying and integrating moment when everything finally makes sense. Calling may come to a person when he or she is reading Scripture or a devotional narrative and recognizes that the experience mirrors his or her own: "That's me!"

Calling may come to some as a direct invitation from another person. Gifts, temperament, spirit, interest, and personality—the community or a person of influence takes note of all of these when asking someone, "Have you ever considered going into ministry?" The call may come as a shock, an unmistakable experience of the divine that precipitates *metanoia* and confirms the person's election to a particular vocation by the voice of God.

In the official processes of the church and as a result of some sense of calling, a person will find a pastoral mentor or be assigned to one. In some persons, the sense of call is clear, articulate, detailed, and exhibiting direction and deep grounding in spiritual understanding. In other people, to simply arrive is enough. They somehow know that what they have experienced, felt, or wondered needs a shepherd of some sort to walk with them in this. The beginning of a mentoring relationship can be clear; or it can be as undefined as "Hush, somebody's callin' mah name. What shall I do?" The question is either assuredly rhetorical or unsettlingly stirring.

It may seem evident that the mentoring relationship begins in the shared experience of call. Whether our callings come in the same manner or means, the assurance of them is what binds us in relationship. More to the point, it is the source of the call—God—who is the primary partner and author of the relationship. Therefore, it is important to recognize the mentoring relationship as a mutual journey in faith with the expectation and promise that the faith and knowledge of God of each member of the partnership will be increased and transformed in the process.

Articulating the Call as Response and Thanksgiving to God

"Can they articulate their call?" This is the question and concern supervising committees, evaluative groups, the church's examining agencies, and the seminaries ask most often. In expounding on the definition of call in the *Discipline* (paragraph 301), the book *Clergy Mentoring* notes, "Speaking and reflecting on one's call is the foundation for vocation as clergy."[2]

The experience of call sharpens an awareness and definition of identity. It is experienced as something with a source and purpose beyond the self. In the Christian context, calling also offers the affirmation of belonging to God and having a part in the divine vocation. We find again and again in the stories related in this book the realization and affirmation of baptismal identity, the gifts of grace, and focused realization of vocation. It is a crucial touchstone of the journey into vocation to articulate that realization and affirmation. The mentoring task is to help find the most accurate description of call—to tell the story of a person's life and experience within which the calling makes sense. Articulation is the capacity of the one called to make his or her experience and understanding comprehensible to another. Words and their meanings are the chief instruments for translating life experience and its wisdom, faith and its grace, hopes and their substance to articulate the deepest sense of what God has done.

Just as the *Logos,* the Word, brought comprehensibility out of the chaos and filled it with form and meaning, so the process of articulation is inherent in giving form to the comprehensibility and meaning of a person's call (see John's interpretation of Genesis 1). Given our understanding that a particular person's call is part of the general calling of the church to Christ's vocation, the church must have a way to become "acquainted with God's movement in a person's life."[3] This acquaintance must not be casual or vague but must be put as clearly and illuminatingly as possible—so much so that the articulation of a person's call not only ensures knowledge of the person's heart, soul, and faith but also deepens his or her acquaintance and knowledge of God and God's purposes.

Articulation has several meanings that are instructive guides and tests for the quality of voicing one's calling.[4] To articulate something is to distinguish it from other things. What are the distinguishing and *distinctive* features of a person's calling? Was it a "Damascus Road" experience? If the awareness of call dawned gradually, can the person trace the distinguishing landmarks in the journey? If it came as an illumination, can he or she provide guidance to the source of light and the distinguishing marks of what was seen? If the call was received through the urging or questioning of pastors, friends, or family, how did the person appropriate the call? A mentor must listen and nurture the distinctive and genuine voice of the mentee to express the call. This may not come easily or all at once. For some persons, mysteries need to be explored; these persons may experience disbelief in what is happening, which requires a leap of faith or forgiveness and affirmation. For others, there is the need for catechesis to teach a greater knowledge of God. The mentor must seek *clarity* and *fullness* in the expression of call. As this is developed and explored together, greater knowledge and understanding of God and God's ways should arise. The mentoring relationship precipitates a greater commitment to discipleship and a yearning to be clear and edifying in one's testimony. In relationship to call, the continuing search for the word(s) brings form to the void(s) in our experience and understanding, and order out of the chaos of what many experience as a confusing and life-shaking experience.

In order to be articulate, the expression of call must form a *coherent whole*. The call must have an internal consistency and integrity and also be coherent in a wider fashion. The integrity of the articulation of call is contingent on its relationship to a person's life and behavior. A person's call is not a credential or an achievement that is accomplished and duly noted as a requirement for successful candidacy. The expression of call should frame, illuminate, and express the person's heart and soul, his or her driving passion and commitment of gifts and resources, and that which makes his or her life comprehensible.

To borrow a definition from the medical field, articulation is a *joint* that brings two portions of the body together. Articulating a person's Christian calling is a critical part of renewing the body of Christ and building up the church. It connects the particular vocation of the one called to the general vocation of the church. Candidates for ministry often express frustration about their "connection" or "communication" with examining agencies. Likewise, field education students have trouble communicating theologically in certain situations of ministry while doing field education. This is an area that needs particular attention and careful shepherding.

An important skill to be developed in all constituents in this process is active listening. It is as important to articulation as clarity of speech or consistent behavior, especially in a world where believers from around the globe gather in a particular place. In such a place, it is the cherished diversity of culture, language, understanding, and faith expression that frame patterns of communication and relationship. Listening, willingness to translate, inquiry for clarification, interpretation for understanding—all are important virtues that must be brought to the engagement of *joining* the call of one to the general call and vocation of the church.

A final definition of articulation comes from the field of architecture. It has to do with giving *visible, clear,* and *concrete expression* to an architectural form. Although we cherish words, we doubt their accuracy unless there is something "concrete" or "physical" that translates them into action. Preaching is verified in practice, so to speak.

I have worked with many candidates for ministry and seminary students on the process of articulation. It is a sacred journey that never ceases to inspire awe at the wonder of God's love and empowering claim on our lives. Commitment to take that journey requires the gifts of patience and encouragement, of faith, and of being open to new ways and understandings of how someone articulates and expresses his or her calling in a manner that edifies and humbles. The sexton at a church where I was pastor taught me a great deal about the landmarks of articulation and the way in which they can come together in a person who had claimed his calling, not in the "finely educated" words often assumed by the term but in the visible, clear, concrete, and distinctive expression of the word he embraced as his own.

Byron had been retired for a decade or more when I arrived as pastor of the church. I noticed that every morning he would unlock the church for the day care and lock it back up in the evening. He arrived early in the morning and stayed until everyone was gone. He always entered the sanc-tuary late in the service and left right after the sermon. He greeted every-one on the way in and said good-bye to everyone on the way out. He seemed like a rather shy man, but he did this public task anyway.

After I had been there a few months, we found time to sit and talk at some length. (Earlier, every time I sought him out for conversation, he had something else to do.) I began the conversation, "Byron, I hear you were a milkman."

"Thought I was; wasn't really. Just delivered milk. Fifty years. Every morning before the sun came up."

"Fifty years, delivering milk. And you weren't a milkman?"

"Nope. Thought I was. But I wasn't."

"Well, then, what *were* you?"

"It wasn't who I *was*; it's who I *am*. You should know that."

I was a little stung by that, but he was as gentle and direct as many "old codgers" were who had formed the spiritual and temporal backbone of the churches I served. I told him that I wanted to hear more.

"I needed some extra money when the kids were growing up, so I took a job as the church sexton. Came here right after my delivery route. My wife keeps after me to retire from this too—bad heart, two bum knees."

He got up from his chair and walked me to the church kitchen, where I learned that he kept a stash of cookies and other goodies his diet wouldn't allow him. From the back of the cabinet he took an old Bible.

"One of the kids left this behind one Sunday. I have been meaning to give it back." He opened to a well-worn page in the Psalms—Psalm 84:10: "For a day in your courts is better than a thousand elsewhere. I would rather be a doorkeeper in the house of my God than live in the tents of wickedness."

I began to understand. He led me to the mechanical room and opened an access door to some ductwork that had been put in for air con-ditioning but never used. Twigs, straw, and scraps of material lined the bottom. "Trustees would want that cleaned out if they saw it, but I won't let 'em." He winked. "'Even the sparrow finds a home, and the swallow a nest for herself, where she may lay her young, at your altars, O LORD of hosts'" (Ps. 84:3).

Byron was not a milkman. He *delivered* milk. His calling had been illuminated in his reading of Psalm 84 when his back had begun to ache from picking up after Sunday school. He sat down in a chair and began to thumb through and read where his eye landed. He was not a milkman. He was the doorkeeper in the house of the Lord. When he read that verse, he was clear about who he was and what he was supposed to devote his life to. It shaped his days. The nests for the birds were an expression of God's claim on his vocation; but even more important was his dedication to making the church the place for which its members and constituents would "long, indeed faint" and think of the church as the "lovely courts" of God.

Byron never did retire, although he accepted the assistance of someone who could do "the heavy lifting." He greeted the congregation on the last Sunday before he died. "Glad you found your way home!" Shortly after he died, the church council gathered to honor him. They had a ceremonial key struck in Byron's honor that today bears his name. The head of the key bears the seal of the church and one side of the shank is inscribed with his name. The words "Psalm 84" are imprinted on the other side. The key is presented as a sign of commissioning to each new chair of the trustees. In making the first presentation, the chair of the church council blessed the gathered congregation, "May each of us have the blessing to be as clear about who we are and what we are doing for God as our dear friend, Byron, and may the hospitality and love he had for this church and its people be shared in heaven as warmly as it was on earth."

In a clear and simple way Byron exemplified the task and blessing of the mentoring partnership: to articulate the call, joining the story of the one who is called to the larger story and context of the people of faith. In so doing, the articulation of call gives glory to God and is a gift to God's people as part of the general vocation of the gathered community. Further, the articulation of call must also have the potential of being edifying to the faith of others. In other words, glorifying God is not simply a private, devotional matter. Nor is its purpose to draw attention to the one who is called. The articulation of call must have the potential of being edifying as it brings others to be renewed and quickened in their faith and understanding of the ways of God.

A sense of call and its dynamism is a lifetime engagement with God. It claims and transforms us in its articulation. The life witness of many of our United Methodist bishops has exemplified the ongoing discipline of discerning, clarifying, and articulating their call as they move from the active general superintendency to chaplaincy at a United Methodist seminary, working with a particular mission project, serving as full-time grandparent, or engaging in myriad other callings. Articulating one's call means struggling with the questions, "Who am I? What is God calling me to do? What gifts do I have that God desires me to use? Hush, let me hear my name."

Transformation of the Call

In the vocation of Christ, we become new persons altogether. Part of the wonderful and awesome opportunity in the mentoring partnership is to witness the transformation worked in the life of a person by the Holy Spirit. It is to be present as a midwife to encourage the new person in Christ to be born. Scripture testifies that calling is often accompanied by the changing of one's name, signifying the new person. When God claimed them for the vocation of being the parents of generations of the covenant, Sarai became Sarah and Abram became Abraham (Gen. 17). Jacob became the namesake of the covenant nation, Israel (Gen. 32). When the vocation of Cephas was focused as the foundation upon which Jesus would build his church and entrust the keys, he was called Peter (Matt. 16:13–19).

I have been blessed by walking with a baker who was transformed and lived his vocation as part of "the bread of life." His engagement in *koinonia* mentoring helped frame his work as vocation so that it reached beyond the bakery and the perishable. It also reached beyond the sectarianism of the church to embrace the town in mission—an imperishable work and a road that led to life. Disheartened by the number of Christmas trees that were simply dumped at the end of the season, the baker had a vision: from these dead trees could come new life . . . the bread of life. Invitations went out from the bakery and the church to the households in town and were also handed to customers in the bakery to make a reservation to have their Christmas trees picked up by the church. Over three weekends in January, teams went out from the church to pick up the trees. They transported truckloads of trees to a chipper for mulching. The invitation asked people to attach an offering to the trees they were discarding. This money would build roofs for churches in Zimbabwe that served as feeding centers for children, orphanages, and AIDS hostels. Hundreds of households participated. Stories were told of non-Christians seeking out their neighbors to see if they had an extra "dead tree" to borrow for the project. It became a yearly event; and the churches received their roofs, protecting the neediest and most vulnerable from the scorching sun and exposure.

A baker was transformed to the vocation of distributing the bread of life. His vision and calling and the organization of the church brought together a town in mission. As his pastor, it was my privilege to mentor him through this transformation and listen to him as he grew into greater fullness of the scope of that vocation. I was blessed to have been part of the various projects that this bread-of-life baker led. I heard him sing, "Bread of heaven, feed me till I want no more" and articulate in visible, connective, and concrete ways the vocation in which he had been divinely identified.

Thus far, I have devoted special and careful attention to the discernment of call and the process of transformation in the lives of those who have been called to the leadership of the church. I hope that in so doing I have not diminished the importance of the process into ordained ministry. From the formation of the priesthood, the school of the prophets and the rabbinate in the Hebrew Bible, to the call of the apostles and the formation of the orders of ministry in the Pastoral Epistles, great care has been given to the leadership of the people of God. As they engage in the work of vocational discernment and empowerment, pastors need keen perception and sensitivity in order to identify and affirm particular gifts and graces that have promise for ordained leadership in the church.

The separation between the ordained and the laity experienced in the church oftentimes falsely relegates an "authentic calling" to the ordained only. Many folks in the church do not make the connexion between those who are deacons and elders and the general ministry of the church. Consequently, the connexion between baptism, vocation, and ordination has been strained, perhaps even severed. In many places, the culture of the call has been less than vital. When I preached a sermon on the call to ordained ministry in one of the churches I served, the response of one parent crystallized the point: "Ministers come from someplace else! They don't come from here!"

Pastors and mentors help open the avenues of response to God's calling. They also have the responsibility of helping to remove roadblocks and to encourage a giving over of oneself to embrace the gifts God has given and decide to fulfill the vocation that uses those gifts most fully.

Karin enrolled to study for a major in sacred music. She had great gifts as a teacher of music and a love of the church. She sought to move from teaching in the public schools to directing a music program in the church. There was a position at the church for her to explore her calling. It became clear that she had extraordinary gifts and interest in the spiritual lives of the folks with whom she worked, taking time to care for them and minister to their pastoral needs. Her opening devotions with the choir were penetrating and converting sermons. Both her mentor in the music area and I spontaneously commented to each other that, in addition to her great gifts for music ministry, Karin had gifts for pastoral ministry.

The reflection came as a surprise to Karin—actually, more like a shock. "They," not she, became pastors, she observed. It was difficult for her to hear what we had seen. I asked Karin to rearticulate her sense of call and what gifts she believed God had called and claimed in her. The narrative clearly included music, but it was filled with the joy and hope that came through the relationship with students and others in her teaching and work at the church. As she told her story again and articulated it another time, I asked her to listen to herself and the words and images that brought the most vitality and joy.

Over the next weeks and months, Karin articulated and rearticulated her sense of calling. She surrounded herself with the biblical narrative and events in the life of the church to help her frame and understand her calling more clearly. One day she related a troubling discovery. She had wanted to be a music director in the church; but a friend who was on the same track told how he discovered that when he played or directed, the music was his gift to God and God's people. It was his "ultimate expression of faith."

"And?" I asked her.

Karin discovered that her joy came when she was with folks in situations of pastoral care and ministry—those times during choir practice when members would talk to her about family and faith. For her, music had become a way to get to the sharing. She also had found her voice as a preacher. She arrived at seminary and the church wanting to be transformed in a certain way; but through our mentoring companionship, Karin was able to allow herself to be open to the working of God's grace to be transforming of her gifts and graces in areas she had not considered. She allowed herself to hear God's voice calling her gifts to the place where her joy and passion were the fullest and most vibrant. Difficult as that was at first to imagine or think, Karin was transformed by grace and was called by a new name, "Pastor." Her ministry has borne great and unexpected fruit.

Todd had been a successful medical doctor for a long time. His practice thrived. He was a faithful member of the church. Over many years he enriched his faith by taking courses at seminary in intensive spurts. The evolution of the medical profession was becoming more and more discordant with his sense of who he was supposed to be as a doctor and his mission as a Christian. However, "doctor" is a powerful identifier of who one is and one's role in society. Over many years, the mentoring relationship walked the journey of identity and vocation, opening the door to the ministry of a United Methodist deacon. Todd's focus and vocation became that of connecting the church and the world in medical ministry to the marginalized and those in need. His identity and ordination to Word and Service—connecting the witness of the church, the justice and healing ministry commissioned by Christ, and the full use of his gifts with the poor and needy—were a transforming and vitalizing fulfillment of the eternal purpose and meaning of Todd's life.

Anne Roberts was the first person I had the privilege to mentor into ordained ministry. She has just recently retired. She came to maturity at a time when "women" and "ordained ministry" did not go together. So when she felt the strong pull to the church, she had no words or understanding even to begin to articulate the feelings and stirrings inside her. Anne was an accomplished organist at a young age and felt that this must have been what the stirrings were all about. However, the audiologist diagnosed her with a condition that would render her hearing more and more compromised until she would lose it altogether. Anne went to college and became a successful public schoolteacher. She was active in the church and the community and in her family and their interests. She was settled in her career and family—until the charge conference that endorsed a young woman student from the nearby college for candidacy as an ordained minister.

I watched Anne during the gathering and noticed that she looked mortified. Concerned, I visited with her. Something had died within her, she said, and something else that she *thought* had died was reborn. The affirmation of the young woman's candidacy had given Anne permission to feel those stirrings again after nearly half a lifetime and to articulate them. In working through the distinctiveness of her call, as she clarified its depth, height, breadth, and length, Anne moved through the limitations that cultural constraints, presumed limitations, and the risk of faithful change had put in her path to fulfill the long-dormant fullness of her calling. She had lived a response that was but an echo until the day when she heard her calling in the fullness of what it could become. Anne recently retired from active itinerant ministry as a cherished colleague, pastor, and mentor to others in their Christian vocation.

The touchstone of call is well worn in the mentoring process. It is to be visited often. Articulation and rearticulation are important for the vital living of every day and the decisions each of us makes to fulfill the vocation for which God has claimed us. I am constantly reminded of the clarity with which Jesus articulated his call and vocation to the Canaanite woman: "I was sent only to the lost sheep of the house of Israel" (Matt. 15:24). How grateful we are that the mentoring of that woman and Jesus' ministry rearticulated his call in the witness and teaching of his life. However, the clearest articulation is the one that binds *all* Christians in the vocation of Christ: "All authority in heaven and on earth has been given to me. Go therefore and make disciples of all nations, baptizing them in the name of the Father and of the Son and of the Holy Spirit, and teaching them to obey everything that I have commanded you. And remember, I am with you always, to the end of the age" (Matt. 28:18–20).

116

Covenant

I am no longer my own, but thine.
Put me to what thou wilt, rank me with whom thou wilt.
Put me to doing, put me to suffering.
Let me be employed by thee or laid aside for thee,
exalted for thee or brought low for thee.
Let me be full, let me be empty.
Let me have all things, let me have nothing.
I freely and heartily yield all things
to thy pleasure and disposal.
And now, O glorious and blessed God,
Father, Son, and Holy Spirit,
thou art mine, and I am thine. So be it.
And the covenant which I have made on earth,
let it be ratified in heaven.[5]

Remember Your Baptism and Its Commission Again

In a brief, terse homily on baptism, Ephraim the Syrian reminds us that our baptismal vocation is a covenant of both identity *and* action. "Thou wast baptized in His Name; confess His name!"[6] Ephraim is emphatic in this sermon that baptism is done *to* us and advocates that we must do something *with* it.

John Wesley drew deeply on the spirituality and theology of the early church in his understanding of the connexion between call, baptism, and covenant.[7] St. John Chrysostom, in his final instructions to baptisands, laid out the life they were to take on in the covenant they were about to accept sacramentally. "Soon you will put on Christ. You must act and deliberate in all things with the knowledge that He is with you every-where."[8] Like Chrysostom, Wesley saw baptism as the "ordinary" means by which a person was incorporated into the body of Christ. His mentor-ing discipline for the Methodists was intended to discern the covenant's "extraordinary" implications for the life of the baptized Christian. Baptism is ordinary in that it is a sacramental symbol and sign of new life in Jesus Christ instituted through the church. The baptismal covenant becomes extraordinary when a person recognizes, embraces, is regenerated,

117

or is born again by a faithful appropriation of or response to Christ's pre-venient, saving grace. All along the faith journey, the church is obligated to provide the baptized with the environments and opportunities to become aware of the covenant in which they have been bound and whose vocational inheritance is theirs to live out.

The importance of knowing the covenants of the faith and living into them, as well as being empowered by them, is critical to understanding and responding to call. The Methodist tradition has been focused on this relationship and empowerment since its inception. As we consider the content of the mentoring relationship, it is important to understand that the issue of covenant may be to focus the implications of the covenants in particular vocational contexts; or it may be that a mentor will need to articulate and teach the covenants as a foundation from which focus and appropriation must take place. The Methodist heritage has been devoted to acquainting persons with the covenant the church shares in Jesus Christ. Further, the mentoring work of the class meeting was intended to help people appropriate the covenant in their own lives. Continued in the work of the Sunday school, youth groups, and other church gatherings for communal and spiritual growth, the effort has been to provide a whole range of experiences that will be means of coming into contact with the grace of God. Focusing on the claim and commissioning of baptism from childhood through adulthood is crucial to the baptismal covenant work of the church.

In 1880, Rev. O. P. Fitzgerald wrote a brief, yet passionate chapter about the nurture of young people in the awareness of their covenant in Christ. The urgency and importance of this agenda bristle in his prose. He was defending the idea that even children would thrive as a result of a class meeting experience.

> As matters now stand, a large proportion of young persons, on joining the Church, have nearly everything to learn with regard to its forms, usages, and activities. Some come from irreligious families in which they have had no opportunity to learn any thing of religious matters. Even the children of religious parents often exhibit astonishing ignorance of these things. The home influence and instruction are too mild to leave any strong and lasting impressions upon their minds. They are never taught what are the doctrines, government, and history of their Church.

They never read a chapter of its Book of Discipline. They have heard but little religious conversation, and that little has been of conventional and fragmentary nature. They have little or no knowledge of religion, except that which they have heard from the pulpit, or absorbed by casual contact with religious people and religious literature. Confined to the routine of attendance on Sunday-preaching, where they hear two sermons, and the weekly prayer-meeting, where they hear a chapter read from the Bible, and listen to two or three prayers by their seniors, what development of spiritual gifts or increase of spiritual life can be expected? They take their places with the dumb and half-alive throngs whose names swell the census of Church-members, but who are scarcely more felt in the way of Christian influence than so many men of straw. The glow of their first love cools. The current of their religious life ceases to flow, and becomes a dead sea without a ripple of fresh spiritual impulse, or aspiration, or energy. What they want is the Class-meeting. There they will find expression and enlargement of their religious thought. There they will enjoy the inestimable advantage to be derived from the wise counsels and warm sympathies of holy men and women who have studied heavenly things in the light of the Bible and in the school of experience. There they learn the language of Zion, and in the freedom of that sacred circle they are trained for service in all the devotional exercises in which the followers of Jesus testify for him and work for the salvation of souls. A great company of living witnesses, devout men and women, who began their Christian courses before Class-meeting waned, would testify that to it more than to any and all other means of grace they are indebted for the influence that gave stability, practical direction, vigor, and joy to their lives. In answer to direct inquiry, the writer has heard this testimony from so many of the strong men and holy women of the generation now passing off the stage, that he cannot doubt the truth of the sweeping statement made in the foregoing sentence.[9]

Mentors Are a Sign and Presence of the Covenant

Dietrich Bonhoeffer helps us focus more sharply the mentoring response to call in the context of covenant. His lifelong quest in discipleship and theological discourse was the concrete expression of God's activity and the covenant of the Christian faith. He was clear that God had formed the new covenant in Christ with the most extreme offering of God's self in

Christ's death; and we are bound in that extraordinary covenant in which we "share in the baptism of his death and resurrection."[10]

Bonhoeffer said that when Jesus calls a person, he bids that person to "come and die." The life-giving, life-claiming covenants held as sacred by the church and set out in Scripture and tradition must be the focus in the mentoring relationship for framing a person's response to call. These covenants frame the response and must be considered formative to a person's appropriation and inclusion in them. For Bonhoeffer, the key question for those who respond to the divine call is to hear what Christ wants us to be and do in the world—and that not for our own sake but for the sake of the world for which he died.[11] In other words, the covenants we embrace—and that embrace us—call us to radical discipleship for the sake of God's mission.

Like Moses with the Hebrew children in the wilderness, the mentor is a sign of the covenant in the context of the relationship (Deut. 4:1–14). Through the difficult years of wandering, doubt, grumbling, revolt, faith-lessness, and petty concerns, Moses kept the covenant with the God of Israel before the people. In his leadership and testimony, Moses kept the relationship between God and God's people ever before them. It was the promise of entering the land given to Sarah and Abraham and the other ancestors as an inheritance that constituted the hope, the inspiration, and the compulsion for enduring the rigors of the wilderness. The substance of those years in the wilderness was not idle wandering or being lost due to lack of direction. The time between being called out of Egypt and entry into the Promised Land was so the Hebrew people could appropriate and enflesh the ten words of God given at Sinai for daily living in community. They acknowledged that being bound in sacred covenant with God would mean a different kind of life than they had seen, learned, and left in Egypt. They were not simply free from bondage or free from Egypt. Within the covenant God made at Sinai, they were a chosen, set-apart people with obligations and observances that responded to the covenant loyalty of God.

A crucial distinction between Christian mentoring and other professional forms of mentoring is the covenant in which Christians are bound. The process of mentoring into Christian vocation is not merely an assessment of skills and aptitudes alone, although these are helpful in discerning particular vocational directions (1 Cor. 12). The environment of mentoring into Christian vocation is the covenant with God. The mentoring partnership is much like the wilderness wandering in that it seeks to enflesh the meaning of the covenant in the life and vocation of the mentee. Like the covenants of the Hebrew people, God has offered to be bound to us in a promise. We see this clearly in the oath given to Sarah and Abraham that promised them numerous offspring and the formation of a great nation (Gen. 17)—an oath renewed to King David and the people. Like the covenants of the Hebrew people, God has bound us in covenant and requires faithfulness in life and work. Christians are bound in the new covenant, the *mandatum novum,* promised in baptism and renewed each time we gather for Eucharist. God's dedication to the oath God took is revealed in the crucifixion of Christ. It was the pledge of the life of God, sacrificed on Calvary. Our response in covenant, also experienced in Christ on Calvary, is the offering of our own lives to the covenant. "We share in the baptism of his death and resurrection." Christ is the new covenant in which we are bound to God and God to us. How then shall we live? What then shall we do?

Mentoring a person into Christian vocation is a sign of a covenant in which the mentee is asked to give his or her life. It is a covenant that a mentor holds before the relationship as one for which Christ gave his life. This is the work of life itself. It requires dedication, care, and intentional preparation through prayer, listening, study, and reflection. I have shared with many mentors and pastors that our work is no less a matter of life (or death) than that of the most skilled surgeon.

I turn once more to Bonhoeffer to remind us of the importance of this critical role of the mentor. Bonhoeffer guides us through the meaning and claim of grace upon our lives. For those who are the spiritual children of the Wesleys and the Methodist movement, the importance of grace is central. The dramatic events of God's prevenient grace and our response to it are at the core of the life of Christ in the world through the Holy Spirit and demand the full attention of the church. That is the organizing principle of the early Methodist movement in the class meeting and the heart of vocational mentoring work, especially in the establishment of clergy mentoring and candidacy mentoring.

Cheap grace is the preaching of forgiveness without requiring repentance, . . . absolution without personal confession. Cheap grace is grace without . . . the cross, . . . [or] Jesus Christ. . . . Costly grace is the gospel, which must be *sought* again and again, the gift which must be *asked* for, the door at which [one] must *knock*. . . . Such grace is *costly* because it calls us to follow . . . *Jesus Christ*. Above all, it is *costly* because it cost God the life of his Son: "ye were bought at a price," and what has cost God much cannot be cheap for us.[12]

In the covenant of Christian vocation, the journey is a growing understanding and committed response to the grace of God. Mentoring a person into clergy leadership in the church is to be intentional about the public character and role that will be required both within the church and in the wider world. Mentoring partnerships join the wilderness wanderings of the church as we move from resurrection to fulfillment. There has already been a great deal of wilderness work done by the church, and we become part of the heritage of that work. It is not new with us, but it is renewed in us. Wilderness work has the promise of refreshing springs in the desert that vitalizes the covenant response in us. It also promises manna from heaven that particularizes the covenant in each of us.

Mentoring work answers the inherent question of the apostle Paul, "What shall we do in the *meantime?*" The mentoring partnership must be a place of formation and *praxis* around response to the covenants of God within the community of the church in the world. It is a place to discern gifts and graces for leadership and occupation. The question, "What shall we do in the meantime?" keeps the focus on Christ and the promise of fulfillment but also reminds us that there is a task and purpose for our life right now within the providence, economy, and vocation of God.

The Methodist Church of Southern Africa invited me to itinerate throughout the connexion in summer 2004. I taught workshops on clergy mentoring but also reacquainted myself with a church, a people, and a land that had changed dramatically since my initial itineration during the final years of the struggle for freedom from apartheid. At that time the predominant covenant was the promise of liberation from the bondage of the oppressive racial system that had blighted the land and threatened to suffocate a people. The church was vibrant in its work and proclamation in freedom's struggle.

This was a new day. Liberation had come, but the issues of poverty, crime, AIDS, and numerous social ills had frustrated many of the clergy with whom I met. They remembered the assurance of the focus of the covenant in the move toward freedom; but now that freedom had come and apartheid had been overthrown, they found themselves in a time beyond the struggle for freedom but before the fulfillment of the vision of a just "promised land." We spoke of it as wilderness time and embraced the pastoral challenge as keeping the vision and promise before the people and doing the difficult "in the meantime" work. I cherish the reflection of one of my colleagues: "Perhaps it will take forty years. Well, there is hope in that."

Several years before the trip I was having lunch with a church member who is an international economist and was doing consulting work for the government and financial leaders in South Africa. Upon returning from one of his trips, he invited me to the faculty dining room, overlooking the resplendent beauty of the Charles River from the elegant confines of Harvard University. He had accumulated and sifted the economic data, crime statistics, HIV/AIDS infection rates, and the like, and had reviewed these with leaders on both sides of the ocean. He was very pessimistic about the future. He had worked the formulas and indicators in a variety of ways; they didn't look good.

"Did you include the faith of the people in your calculations?" I asked him gently.

It was an absurd idea to him. But I reminded him that the church and the hopeful promise of liberation were a crucial focus for sustaining the people through the long years of oppression and the transition to a new nation. I wondered with him what it would mean to look at the future hope of the people with a focus on the promise of Christ. Such an act of imagination did not deny the economic considerations, but it embraced the work of an economist in the vocation of Christ, if only for a moment over dessert. It invited a member of the church to join in the wilderness wanderings of the people he sought to resource and to be bound with them in the covenant he and they shared through baptism. It was to reorder the covenants and their claims in the consideration, meaning, and focus of his work.

At another luncheon, he told me of his travels to China and the concern about ecological challenges, population growth, and other issues confronting an emerging new economy and society. Before I had a chance to say anything, he looked at me and his face broke out into a large grin. Rising slightly in his chair, he said with a flamboyant gesture, "I know, I know, the solution has to do with God or something!" Then he settled back into his chair and engaged a serious, reflective tone that searched his memory and the teachings of his faith. "But what?" he wondered.

The mentor is a living witness and articulate presence of the covenants that bind us to God and to the church and that frame our vocation.

Conflict and Confirmation

Mentors and mentees often walk through the dangerous wilderness of competing and conflicting covenants that threaten to tear at them and pull them in a variety of directions, identities, and commitments. These are imperative considerations for the mentoring partnership to consider. They cannot be treated lightly. John's Gospel remembers the danger of poisonous serpents in the wilderness that plague the journey (Num. 21:8–9); yet John reminds us of the importance of keeping our focus on Christ as the one who reconciles (John 3:11–16).

Many similar conflicts and confusions of covenant confront the transforming work of the wilderness. Let me lay out some of these in the context of candidacy and clergy mentoring in The United Methodist Church.

One example is the covenant of marriage and family. It is critical to consider this covenant during the candidacy process.[13] Marriage is an exclusive, sanctified covenant in the church. It requires of two people to give themselves to each other and to assume a new identity, as well as to establish a new family as a result of the oaths and vows they make with one another.

Ordination requires a giving of oneself fully to ministry. It means joining an order and giving oneself over to the authority of a bishop, the community of others in the order, and other clergy.[14] The demands of the covenant of ministry and the covenant of marriage and family often conflict in terms of presence, attention, expectations, and mobility. The life given to the covenant of marriage and family often is subordinated, in whole or in part, to the demands of pastoral ministry. Alternatively, the ire of the congregation or other agency of the church is stirred because the clergyperson seems "unavailable." The stories and examples are too many to even begin to recount here. However, the mentee who seeks to move into ordained ministry needs to address and begin to appropriate these concerns in his or her life. Divorce and/or withdrawal from active ministry are often the evidence of the difficulty of negotiating these covenants, both cherished by the church.

Many of my students and mentees who are single, or who are divorced and choose not to remarry, find the conflict between the perceived image of a pastoral leader in the church as a selfless, sexless person, on the one hand, and their desire to live into the fullness of their humanity by dating or attending to deep friendships or by investing solitary time in the disciplines of celibacy, on the other, difficult to negotiate. Expectations of time, presence, and commitment to the church on the part of members often militate against the ability to spend time developing personal relationships.

Others who feel called to leadership in the church, especially into the ordained ministry, but whose sexual orientation is not embraced because it is deemed "incompatible with Christian teaching" consider themselves in a place where the church denies the call they have received and the covenant for which they are willing to give their lives. The matter is confused further by the meaning of the inclusive covenant the church seeks to extend "to be in ministry for and with all persons," especially in light of the similar claim about those of differing sexual orientations being of "sacred worth." To those who understand their sexual orientation as a gift from God and an inextricable part of their personhood, the church's official stance—declaring them of sacred worth, while considering the practice of homosexuality as "incompatible with Christian teaching"—is a painful and excluding contradiction.[15]

Sorting through the issues and demands at the outset of a person's journey into vocation is not enough. It is a lifelong demand that all too often does not receive the necessary mentoring until fractures and fissures occur within a person and in the covenants in which he or she is bound. By then the serpent's fangs have done their damage, and an active mentoring relationship loses the focus on the partnership and how to live out of the covenants that mentor and mentee have made in Christ Jesus.

In this regard, the mentoring partnership functions much like the reminders of covenant required in the Shema: "Recite them to your children and talk about them when you are at home and when you are away, when you lie down and when you rise. Bind them as a sign on your hand, fix them as an emblem on your forehead, and write them on the doorposts of your house and on your gates" (Deut. 6:7–9).

Candidacy and Clergy Mentors Are the Presence of the Orders of Ministry

Among individuals discerning their Christian vocation in covenant, some respond to a ministry that is set apart in the church for ordained or licensed leadership. The mentor who is assigned to a mentee for the particular role of candidacy or clergy mentoring represents the covenant of ministry and the orders of The United Methodist Church. An important part of this process is to focus on the particular call and covenant, always remembering that this call and covenant are situated within the baptismal covenant and call to vocation in Christ. Each order has specific ministries and responsibilities.[16]

These covenants are the work of many generations who have been intent on discerning the meaning of the covenant in which the church is bound. In its living "in the meantime," the church has renewed and refined the profile of leadership in the Pastoral Epistles in order to understand how best to order the church for Christ's mission in the world. United Methodists have done ongoing wilderness work in the area of the general ministry of the church and of the ordained ministry in particular. Some may get frustrated that the work never seems to be completed. The echoes of the frustration in the wilderness and the grumbling of the leaders toward Moses reverberate in our processes today. However, in the meantime, we have covenanted together to live out Christ's commission through the church in specific orders and patterns. In this process within the mentoring relationship it is crucial to keep the focus on the eternal and irrevocable covenant of baptism and its seminal call, claim, and promise.

That is not to say, however, that the covenants of leadership are not important. It is only to remember that these are covenants in which we have bound ourselves in community and are seeking the blessing and empowerment of the Holy Spirit. The church's ongoing attempts at revision and reform of its forms of leadership make this point, yet it remains an extraordinarily difficult task. The exploration of call and covenant in the mentoring relationship will expose the dynamics of the way church communities and polities have appropriated God's covenant and melded it with human traditions and expectations. It is not surprising that the exploration will reveal that some of these expectations and covenants are in conflict or make the initial clarity of a call more confusing in a particular expression of polity or church practice. Testing may yield a rich harvest in the relationship with God and the claim God has made; but it is also important to engage the agreements and understandings of the community or clergy order and the covenants they currently share. Such engagement is difficult and at times can be excruciatingly painful.

Celibacy and maleness are agreements of covenant for entering the priesthood in the Roman Catholic Church. Heterosexuality is an agreement for affirmation in the ordained leadership of The United Methodist Church. Itinerant ministry is an agreement for entry into the order of elders. Each of these agreements defines the covenant the mentor represents in the mentoring relationship. However, it is also critical that the mentor knows the difference between the covenant of Sinai and the wilderness work of the Hebrew people. It is crucial that the mentor knows the covenant of the Cross and the "in-the-meantime" work of the church and allows for a prophetic voice—a voice for the marginalized and the suffering, a voice for the hope of revisioning and the articulation of reformation.

In certain ways the process toward leadership stands over against the wilderness work and the "in-the-meantime" agreements of covenant. It may even become evident that the particular covenant into which a person wishes to be included will not be open or hospitable. However, throughout this book, I have stressed that the primary work of the mentoring partnership is not to help the mentee enter into a particular profession or ecclesiastical confession, important as those are. Rather, the focal work is to attend to as faithful a response as possible to Christ's call and claim in vocation. Such work may include walking with the lone prophet, the Syrophoenician woman, the reformer, or the suffering servant as a humble sign of the covenant of the church, yet taking the risk of faith to leap beyond this wilderness to the fulfillment of the yearned-for promise.

Mentors find themselves before the Jerusalem Council making the case for the Gentiles with the apostle Paul and Barnabas. They often find themselves listening to the covenant received and understood in relationships and ways they had never known or imagined. Mentors are enjoined, recruited, and assigned to accompany persons who are yearning to know the covenant of Christ; but perhaps these persons are from regions not yet known or experiences not yet encountered. Or perhaps they express ways of being Christian that spring from cultures and understandings that heretofore have been considered foreign or unclean. Mentors are often called to do the difficult work of a missionary, an evangelist, and an apostle, to represent the "Gentile" with integrity before the ruling "councils." "Now we see in a mirror, dimly, but then we will see face to face. Now I know only in part; then I will know fully, even as I have been fully known. And now faith, hope, and love abide, these three; and the greatest of these is love" (1 Cor. 13:12–13).

Claiming and Revisioning the Covenant

It is important to articulate a covenant between the partners in the mentoring relationship. Fundamentally, the definitions revolve around these four questions:

1. Who are we? (How have God and the church called us together? What will bind us and what do we have to offer one another and God in this relationship?)
2. Where are we? (At what point do we find ourselves in the journey?)
3. What time is it? (Early and new to the covenant or late and confirmed? Or is this a time in the wilderness? Are we "in the meantime" when revision and renewal is important, much like refreshment in the late afternoon?)
4. Where are we going? (Where are we being led and by whom—God and/or the church and/or another party to the covenant? Are

we wandering or is our journey intentional? What lies along the path?)

I strongly recommend that mentoring partnerships work on the covenant they share as much as they focus on the covenants in which they are bound. Mentoring partnerships are not incidental meetings but are a giving and receiving of the life shared in Christ in a profound offering of one to the other. It is an intentional partnership offered to the ministry, vocation, and glory of God. Particular attention and intentionality are necessary for mentoring to fulfill its promise and to be a faithful witness to the presence of the One who is the author and object of the relationship itself.

When relationships begin to take on the character of vocational mentoring, it is important for participants to voice the informal covenants that exist between them. Those in candidacy mentoring and clergy mentoring as well as other mentoring relationships that are part of the formal covenant of ministry should formulate their relationship in a more formal covenant that respects the disciplines and designs for which the partnership was intended. Throughout this chapter, I have articulated the importance of the mentoring relationship. However, it needs to be acknowledged in the covenantal commitments expressed in the particular covenant made between the participants. Acknowledging the purpose, goals, protocols for meeting, commitments, and time frames is imperative for the effectiveness of mentoring covenants (and reflects the structures of biblical and other faith covenants).

The discipline of expressing the covenant in a formal, written statement within mentoring relationships is required for candidacy and clergy mentors in the United Methodist protocol. This practice is to model the way of God with God's people and the formation of covenant within the faith community. It is a spiritual discipline designed to develop skill in Christian leadership. The discipline for covenanting in the candidacy process is laid out specifically as the foundation for the entire process of preparation for ministry. It reflects the participation of the immediate partners in the relationship but also clearly embraces the active presence of God. Further, the candidacy covenanting process is intentionally grounded in Scripture and the Wesleyan tradition.[17]

The clergy mentoring process of covenant making recommends specific issues that focus on the critical areas of trust and boundaries as well as the importance of the practical details of covenant.

1. How can boundaries of trust and respect be established and maintained?
2. How can the relationship be ended in a respectful manner when either or both participants no longer feel safe because their willingness to be vulnerable has been threatened?
3. What can be done to make sure that sharing the journey of ministry is more important than fixing specific problems?
4. When necessary, how can the mentor "speak the truth in love" regarding effectiveness in ministry in such a way that the mentee feels empowered to face issues head on? There may be instances in which it becomes clear that pursuing ordained ministry is not in the mentee's best interest. In such cases, the mentor should carefully encourage the mentee to explore his or her call and gifts again in order to assist the mentee to consider other appropriate expressions of ministry.

While drafting the covenant, participants should seek agreement on specific issues. These may include the following:

- learning goals (for local pastors enrolled in the Course of Study, the curriculum is part of the focus)
- resources to be used (materials, persons, events)
- shared expectations
- meeting frequency, dates, times, and places
- responsibilities for preparation and follow-up[18]

The work of the mentoring partnership is clearly holy work. It is the focused and intentional labor of the church in the *koinonia* of two who are gathered in the presence of Christ. And it is work that is not done until it finds its end and fulfillment in Christ.

The work of Christian vocational mentoring is wilderness work in that it must accompany the journey through the changing circumstances and experiences of life. Mentors may be chosen for discrete portions of the journey and for specific reasons, but the work of appropriating covenant "in the meantime" does not end until we are with the "church at rest" in the consummation of Christ. Like the revisioning and reappropriating of covenant that thread through the narrative of both Testaments, similar work is always before a person bound in covenant to Christ's vocation. Mentoring companionship enriches and focuses the journey.

Jim had just finished a punishing round of therapy for thyroid cancer. He was the proverbial rocket scientist. He had spent the better part of his career at MIT working on the team that developed the Chandra telescope to be launched on the back of a space shuttle in order to penetrate the universe with X-rays and photograph what Jim referred to as "God's big moment of creation." Jim and his wife, Sophie, had been formative members of the church, dedicating many hours to youth work. They had also been instrumental in forming a network of homeowners who provided hospitality to families whose loved ones had journeyed from out of town for the cutting-edge research and health care provided in the city. They were devoted to the church and the study and witness of the gospel.

It was late afternoon when I arrived at the house to see Jim after his daily therapy. It had exhausted him. During our conversation he indicated that he wondered what God wanted of him now. This man who was a light in science and faith was wandering around a little lost. "I have spent a lifetime wrapping my head around infinity, and I think I have that mastered. I wanted to find God in it." I listened in the long pause. "And I have tried to understand eternity—at least, I thought I understood the faith—but I am having trouble now figuring out where they come together and how I *know*."

We sat for quite a while, listening and trying to find the intersection, wandering around. I came back several times over the next week or so. Jim wound up in the hospital, and I showed up shortly after he was admitted. He had a piece of paper on the side table with a Cartesian plane drawn on it. The axes were labeled "infinity" and "eternity." At the intersection were three words: "Cross = Christ = Hope."

"The cross was right in front of me," he said. "Engineers need schematics, and the cross was right in front of me. The hope part came from you. I figured you must have come so often because you were hoping for something to happen. I wondered what hope you had, and it came to me when I couldn't sleep." He pointed to the words on the paper.

"Now, my pastor and friend, I need to know the substance of Christian hope. I may not have much time left, but I will give you until tomorrow." Jim smiled with encouragement. I spent the evening poring over my resources and concordances, reading the theologians and great spiritual mystics. Jim was asking me to help him get a fix and a focus on an assurance of faith in the difficult days of terminal cancer. It felt rather obvious and perhaps a little trite to bring what my night of searching had yielded: "Faith, hope and love abide; but the greatest of these is love."

Jim's career had been an investment in the concepts and possibilities locked in the mystery of the universe and the boundless reality of God that is beyond most of our capacity to grasp, let alone explore. In the wilderness of cancer and the meantime of the new circumstances of his life, his vocation changed from infinity and eternity to the depths of love divine. He shared that his natural impulse was to withdraw from the world; from his friends; his colleagues; and even his wife, Sophie, to save her the pain of the final phases of his illness and death. In the words of Paul, he found the truth of the dim mirror that represented the future; but he began to live fully in the abiding realities of faith and hope that he found in the investment and nurture of the love he shared with his wife, family, colleagues, and friends. In so doing, his appropriation of the covenant was revised and transformed; his life continued to have purpose and vitality until the moment he drew his last breath. I was present with Sophie in the quietness of that last breath. "I know now what eternity is," I said. "So do I," Sophie whispered amid the tears. "Jim shared it with me."

The mentor must be a faithful companion and keep within his or her witness and partnership the assurance of the exhortation to the Hebrews:

> Do not, therefore, abandon that confidence of yours; it brings a great reward. For you need endurance, so that when you have done the will of God, you may receive what was promised.
>
> For yet "in a very little while,
>   the one who is coming will come and will not delay;
> but my righteous one will live by faith.
>   My soul takes no pleasure in anyone who shrinks back."

But we are not among those who shrink back and so are lost, but among those who have faith and so are saved.

Now faith is the assurance of things hoped for, the conviction of things not seen. Indeed, by faith our ancestors received approval. By faith we understand that the worlds were prepared by the word of God, so that what is seen was made from things that are not visible. (Heb. 10:35–11:3)

Context

The patterns of church had been established in me from the cradle. New England, perhaps more specifically, factory-city Methodism, had permeated my experience of church and had been developed for generations to shape the worship patterns, hymns, behaviors, and identity of being part of the church. I ventured from that environment and experience to the rural Midwest to attend college and secured an appointment as a local pastor at a small rural church during my senior year. I remember the culture shock in my freshman year when those who lived on my floor were comparing the number of traffic lights in their hometowns. The only one who might have had that knowledge in my home city was the administrator of public works. It was not crucial civic knowledge for those leaving home to attend college. I felt like a stranger in a strange land.

Now I was the pastor of a church in a town of one hundred who counted stop signs, not traffic lights. Putnamville did not have mail delivery. Everyone went to the post office. The church mail was special, hand delivered to the pulpit. The percentage of United Methodists in town was the same as the church's membership—eighty-three. United Methodists were the clear majority in town. When charge conference was held, so was the annual town meeting. Both were held in the sanctuary with a simple switch of presiding officers. A strawberry social was held after adjournment (which could be no longer than two hours from the opening prayers). Attendance on Sunday was not much lower than the church membership, and Sunday school attendance was higher. The lay leader of the church had taken me "under his wing" (perhaps the most popular expression for mentoring in those days). He had advised me to make sure that I put plenty of the "old, familiar, singable" hymns in the Sunday service. So I did. Or so I thought.

Several weeks into the fall, he came to me with a look of disappointment on his face. I clearly had chosen the wrong hymns. What hymns should we sing? "Our favorite is 'Come to the Church in the Wildwood.'"

No wonder; we were standing in front of "a little brown church in the vale." Frances got the members of the church to gather around me after the service and teach me the hymn. It was the way they had learned it, by singing it without a book every last Sunday of the month. "There is nothing so dear to my childhood." I looked for it in the old *Methodist Hymnal* but couldn't find it. I was told that it was in a camp songbook; but the folk of the church had taught me the hymn, and that was how I wanted to cherish it. Frances and some of the other members of the church took me under their wing to teach me the culture and context of a small farming community. The second lesson, after "The Church in the Wildwood," had to do with ending the service on time so they could get their tables at the local diner before the Baptists, "who always went long."

More important, I learned how they read Scripture. Being from the city, I had to learn the teachings of Jesus as metaphors and allusions to agrarian life that I could only guess at or read in commentaries written by academics. In the Sunday school class, I listened to how these people read Scripture and how they allowed Scripture to read them. Sheep, goats, seed spreaders, farming, herding, stewardship, and the household—all came alive in a different way for me in this place. These people showed me what a shepherd does and encouraged me to reflect with them on how that shaped my role as pastor. To this day, when I read those passages, I can see, smell, and feel the experiences of those days and how they affected my understanding of ministry.

I was also challenged by the way that church pushed beyond the texts that addressed their agrarian life. The Macedonian call for aid issued by the apostle Paul was their clarion for mission. Although financial resources were not in abundance, they were plentiful in the stewardship of that church—so much so that they dedicated great sums through the United Methodist Committee on Relief and the Advance Specials of the General Board of Global Ministries to fund the building of churches and agricultural development around the world. It was a formative part of their worship and prayer life, Bible study, and spiritual formation as well as administrative and financial concern.

When I left seminary, I was well educated in the liturgical renewal that began to find its way into United Methodist publications and practices in the 1970s. Many of the traditions of my childhood had been challenged and revised in ecumenical conversation. The chanting of psalms and use of ashes on Ash Wednesday, sprinkled water for baptismal renewal, and foot washing on Maundy Thursday were all emphasized as important revisions in United Methodist practice in order to enrich our worship and to allow us to enter more fully into ecumenical Christian practice.

With this formative education in my head and the conviction of its rightness in my soul, I proceeded to implement it in the local church to which I was appointed out of seminary. It all seemed to go well until the imposition of ashes to begin Lent. That was a point when *context* was crucial and important to the worship and pastoral ministry of the congregation.

This congregation was comprised of folks from the town and farms that were nestled in the beautiful Berkshires of Massachusetts. Along with them were employees and some professors of Williams College. Drawn to this location following World War II were young people from Europe, seeking new opportunities and a new life. When the congregation sang certain hymns familiar in their "heart language," the offering of languages was rich.

However, the symbol of ashes was not a uniting harmony. It had been a symbol of painful division between Catholics and Protestants. One of the formative and cherished families in the church was of Huguenot descent. They had survived the war, participating in the rescue of Jews, along with their honored father, a Protestant pastor. These memories were graphic and faith forming. So were the memories of persecution by the Catholic majority during their childhood. It was a cultural divide that had been an undercurrent since the revocation of the Edict of Nantes.

Marc came to me after the Ash Wednesday service filled with deep anger and hurt. Yet he also had the wisdom and patience of those who offer themselves as mentors and companions on the faith journey. He explained that when he was in school in his youth, Ash Wednesday was a difficult day. It was clear who was Catholic and who was Protestant. In the schoolyard one year, "they" wrestled him to the ground and tore off his shoes to see if the stories they had heard were true. They wanted to see whether Protestants really had hooves.

He acknowledged that the unity of the church was important, and I knew that his disposition supported the church's unity and oneness in Christ. But this schoolyard experience had been seared in his memory and those of his family and others with similar experiences in the church as a sign of division and persecution. Understanding the context for practice was imperative.

When it came to planning Maundy Thursday, I wondered whether I should skip the foot-washing piece altogether. My clergy mentor encouraged me to explore it with the congregation and to specifically bring it up with Marc, not assuming what he would say. Marc's initial reaction was much like the response to ashes.

But several days later he came to my office. "Will you wash my feet?"
"Yes," I said.
"Then, I would like you to do that. I have thought about it and what Jesus said when he washed Peter's feet. This will be healing. And then may I wash yours?"

Marc and his wife, Michou, were important mentors to me in those years. They shared the kind of friendship that Christ has called us to. They introduced me to a faith formed in the horror of war and in the face of the Gestapo, transplanted to the bucolic Berkshires. They challenged me to bridge the gulf of the faith journey traveled by Christians and Jews. To that end, they mentored me into an active sharing of ministry with the Jewish community in that setting as well as the churches I served subsequent to those years. And they claimed an identity and a transformation in my leadership that they summed up by honoring me with the title "Rabbi."

Understanding the Text in Context and Letting the Text Read the Context

Frances and others in Putnamville, and Marc and Michou in Williamstown, became more than teachers; they became cultural interpreters and mentors of my growth, understanding, and identity in ministry. This is a crucial element of mentoring a person into vocation. It means considering the importance of context for ministry. It is also the faithfulness of a mentor to be present with a mentee as the context challenges, tests, reshapes, and reforms his or her identity and acuity for vocation. It is often one of the most difficult skills for a mentor to navigate in the personal relationship of mentoring as well as in understanding the impact of context on the entire ecology of the church and a leader's place within it. I often think of these persons as akin to Priscilla's relationship with Paul. It is clear from the text of Acts and the Pauline epistles that Priscilla played an important role in the mission of the early church. With Paul under arrest a great deal of the time, it is not too difficult to make the leap that other people, namely Priscilla and the others mentioned in his correspondence, brought the news and framed the issues of the context. In this way, the Priscillas of Paul's ministry played the vital mentoring role of interpreting and framing the issues of the various congregations with whom Paul was in contact and helped sharpen his understanding and effectiveness.

Space does not allow me to survey the full scope of academic and ecclesiological work done in the area of context. However, let me mention a few resources. The work of Letty Russell and many other feminist writers has focused on the relationship of text and its context from a feminist perspective. Many other theologies of liberation have helped us do similar work from a variety of cultures, perspectives, and contexts. Paul Ricoeur and Walter Brueggemann, along with many writers who are exploring the postmodern world, are grappling with issues of phenomenology, hermeneutics, and metanarrative and their efficacy for reading the text in context and methodologies for the text reading the context. Many ecclesiological observers have worked with the sociology of the church and various models and portals for understanding a variety of cultures and contexts.

The vast number of perspectives offered to the church through authors like these as well as contextual and cultural interpreters are rich resources for the mentoring partnership. There are often commitments and convictions about the importance of context that emerge from one's own journey and study that must find their way into the mentoring relationship. Confronting different and new contexts and ways of

137

living out sacred narratives or sacred texts often enhances one's capacity to challenge, test, and reform one's preconceptions and personal narratives.

It is important to bring the frames we have noted above to the mentoring conversation as well as acknowledge differing theological perspectives and their conflicting hermeneutics.

- Some persons enter the mentoring process without acknowledging that their cultural and ecclesiastical experiences are not universal norms. It is important to articulate and test such assumptions.
- In some dominant and orthodox approaches, the role of context is not as crucial as the unity found in doctrine and doxological practices. This approach shapes the consideration of context that emphasizes how the text reads the context most heavily.
- For approaches focusing on phenomenology and experience, the importance of the reader's location, the preference for the marginalized, and the voices of those who "were closest to the heart of Christ," it is important to embrace a comprehensive understanding of the locus of ministry. The contextual reading of the text and the imperatives of culture are highly valued and emphasized.

Before going to Nicaragua in the early 1980s to work with the *campesinos* in the middle of the Contra War, I read *The Gospel in Solentiname,* as recorded by a Catholic priest, Ernesto Cardenal. He had transcribed the method that "base communities" in Central America use for reading and discussing the scriptural text as radically rooted in the communities' context. In these communities, this discussion substituted for the homily or sermon. I was struck by the profound similarities between this method and the reading and discussing of Scripture in the Sunday school in Putnamville. Yet there were also differences. In the base communities, Christ was "a poor man" and the gospel was read in that context, with the feel and texture of the locale.

I didn't go to Solentiname but to the border town of Jalapa. I stayed with a family of four. The father shared in the farming economy of the village. His wife helped, sold soda from the house, and kept the house. The children were in school, thrilled that they were being taught to read and write in Spanish and English. The eldest, a twelve-year-old girl, produced a Bible and asked me to teach her to read it in English. I agreed, on condition that she would help me with my Spanish.

On the wall of the main room of the house, the only room that had a cement foundation (the others being dirt), she had written a slogan. We began the lesson with her proudly pointing to it. Her parents beamed when she did that. (I am not sure there would have been as much pleasure exhibited by my parents with such a scrawl on the living room wall.) "*Cristo es la roca,*" the slogan read. "Rock," she wrote in chalk. "*Roca.*" She insisted we begin our lesson there.

I understood the importance of the words, "Christ is the rock." We went long into the evening reading the Bible together. She had underlined every image of Christ in the New Testament. We went through them all. In our conversation together she mentored me in the understanding of the contextual reading of Scripture. This twelve-year-old Nicaraguan, who had only just learned to read, expressed a Christology so clear, so biblical, so persuasive, and so rooted in her own context that when she asked me what it meant in English, I found an abject poverty in the sophisticated expression I had brought with me. Although I did not brush aside her desire to know, I felt that it was important for me to hear the divine injunction in those hours, "Be still, know that I am God." And listen—and be transformed.

Mentoring and Cultural Location

The United Methodist Church is experiencing the gift of persons called to ordained ministry from a wide variety of ethnic, cultural, and national backgrounds. This reflects the larger mobility of society and the need for persons to understand their vocation within multicultural contexts. For some time now, the business world has been engaged in the so-called "global economy" and developing strategies to work in various contexts. There are varying degrees to which these are helpful. Yet many persons engaged in mentoring into Christian vocation are less aware of the multicultural dynamics and importance of context and cultural location than their counterparts in the business world. This is a wake-up call, especially given the conviction that Christ is the Savior of the world and that the church is universal.

Mentoring partnerships often take place among persons who have crossed traditional boundaries, bringing to candidacy and clergy mentoring relationships and vocational mentoring in local churches in new, challenging, and enriching ways the rich variety of culture and contexts found in the universal church. The cultural contexts from which persons originate and are formed may be quite different from those in which they will serve in ministry or experience Christian vocation. In generations past, the dominant culture established the norms and practices for institutional conformity and assumed or even imposed a church culture and expectation that mirrored its own. Theology, morality, language, and behavior were uncritically universalized by the dominant culture. This required persons outside the dominant experience, culture, or point of view to put their cultural, racial, ethnic, and national gifts "under a bushel" (at best) and conform to expectations uncritically. This happened not only in cultures that were clearly disparate but also in cultures that exhibited a preference for who got to define what the culture meant and what was considered the norm to which persons conformed. The emergence of the voices of liberation theologians has precipitated a paradigm shift in how the church understands itself. Not only communities finding a clear voice in theologies of liberation but also others whose experience has been marginalized and forgotten have found "their loosened tongues employed."

However, the ripples have not totally reconfigured the landscape or become settled in the geography of the whole church. Attention needs to be paid to the impact of the global nature of the church and the shifting tectonic plates inherent in the perspective of the gathered people of God in the diversity of the community of Christ.

The faith vision of the church and the reality of its experience require an active commitment to discerning the ways in which culture, economic location, race, nationality, and the like are valuable yet varied gifts exercised in ministering the gospel. It is especially essential that in environments in which cross-cultural, cross-racial, and cross-contextual mentoring takes place, a climate of mutual inquiry, learning, and appreciation pervade the relationship. It is also important to acknowledge the mentoring relationship as a seed of transformation in the church—or, to use another vocational metaphor, leaven in the loaf. The mentoring relationship nurtures the call and vocation of a person in ministry preparation and broadens and deepens the faith life of the whole church. Persons involved in the ministry preparation process who seek to move beyond cultural and racial parochialism will also become leaders in fulfilling the vision of *shalom* that is grounded in the gospel of peace, justice, and the healing of Christ.

Lucia Ann McSpadden has done some vital and instructive work for The United Methodist Church in the area of appointment making in cross-cultural and cross-racial contexts.[19] Her gathered wisdom is helpful and provokes those who enter into a mentoring partnership to test their assumptions about their own cultural values and ways of being. As a part of the traditionally identified dominant culture of United Methodism, McSpadden's gathering of a poignant list of Euro-American characteristics reminded me how easy it is to treat these as the fulcrum of judgment in leadership. It also reminds me that these characteristics are not universally embraced. "This culture places high value on *doing* rather than being, on *getting things done* rather than building relationships, on *individual responsibility,* on a *sense of future* as something we can plan for, and on *production and visible results* for which people are expected to be *task oriented* and *achievement focused.*"[20]

I would encourage those who engage in cross-cultural mentoring or who seek to appreciate the wonderful diversity of the church to use McSpadden's work as a companion to the work they are reading. It provides invaluable help and guidance for mentors, supervisors, and leaders in an increasingly diverse church.

Patiently Listening and Seeking a Common Ministry in Christ

The immigrant Korean community in the Berkshires was spread over a large area. While Dr. Sang Ho Lee pastored the church prior to my appointment, he ministered to them in circuit-rider fashion, moving from town to village to house. Some were Christians before arriving in New England; others were converted since their arrival. I had the invaluable opportunity to invite Dr. Lee to teach, empower, and mentor me in pastoral ministry among those who cherished him as their pastor. As we visited in the hospital or made a visit to a family home, we shared with each other how much of a gift it is to have these collegial relationships.

Pastoral ministry can be a solitary task and especially isolating when language and culture seem so impenetrable. Dr. Lee and I took time with each other, seeking understanding and wisdom from each other in terms of what we saw in each other's practice of ministry. It was humbling and enriching. We recognized the importance of patience, the imperative of listening and inquiring, the acknowledgment of limitation, and the inability to translate effectively. However, in those times together, we also found opportunity for blessing and our common commitment to the ministry we shared in Jesus Christ. We were able to learn in ways that are impossible in monocultural relationships and to appreciate Christ's amazing work through the rich diversity of the church. In some ways, I began to see that the concerns expressed around cross-cultural relationships are best understood as important temporal, yet hopefully temporary concerns. The inherent hope in the work to communicate and relate across cultures is to seek a unity in the body of Christ. Our shared culture will be the commitment to effective communication and understanding that unites diversity in the unity of a common and celebrated culture in Christ.

On a recent trip to Korea, I recalled with my hosts the wonderful introduction I had to ministry from a Korean perspective through Dr. Sang Ho Lee. A day later our delegation visited Mokwon University, where Dr. Lee had returned to teach until his retirement. Extraordinary measures had been made in the intervening hours to find Sang Ho and arrange for our reunion seventeen years after we last met. The gift of extreme hospitality at a table that was acknowledged to be the communion of Christ was a renewed gift of Korean culture to the whole body of Christ. When we were ready to depart, Sang Ho took my hands with the gentle blessing I had seen him give so many years ago, yet had not understood. "You are still a very beautiful man. God's blessings go with you and your family." What a wonder to cherish and bless the beauty of the soul that radiates in the countenance and spirit.

The dramatic issues of mentoring outlined above are critical for the future of the church. However, they should not minimize the importance of the subtleties of contextual understanding in settings that seem comfortable and similar. When I first arrived at Putnamville, I locked the door of my car, as was my practice elsewhere. Here it was taken as a sign that I did not trust the people. For me, it was an assurance that my car would not be stolen. Nevertheless, I unlocked my car door; and after worship the car was filled with vegetables. Similarly, moving across town in my home city was a reorientation to what I thought I already knew. Moving from a factory working-class, industrial culture to a church of professionals and executives several miles away, in many ways, was more difficult than moving to a culture considered radically different.

The issues of context are profound and imperative to the task of mentoring. They are often difficult to navigate for both the mentor and the mentee. Yet they are the critical demand of the Christian faith, wherein "the Word became flesh and lived among us" (John 1:14).

Differences in Gender, Race, and Age in the Mentoring Relationship

In addition to cultural location and differences of worldview, other dynamics can impact a mentoring relationship in both subtle and overt ways. Much has been written in the last decades that shed light on these dynamics, especially as a result of the theologies of liberation. It is important to be aware of the issues of power and authority, normative assumptions that may be inaccurate and disruptive of relationships, as well as psychological and relational considerations.

These issues are most pronounced when the mentoring partners are of different genders, come from different racial experiences, or have a great disparity in age. It is imperative to return to the understanding of Christian vocational mentoring in its least hierarchical form and to be reminded that in the relationship of Mentor and Telemachus, the voice of the mentored one is heard only faintly and is of marginal importance. It is crucial that United Methodists embrace the inquisitive and empowering position of the mentoring figure in the *habari gani menta* model, outlined earlier.

There are three practices that I have found helpful or have seen modeled in mentoring relationships where differences in gender, race, or age were present. These practices can enhance the effectiveness of all mentoring relationships, but they are especially poignant in the relationships we are considering here.

The first practice is to remember that the voice and experience of the one being mentored has its own authority and brings an important perspective. Mentors must provide a safe environment in which the partners can seek mutual understanding and critique the limitations placed on identity by racial factors, gender privilege, or age entitlements. It is in honest inquiry and openness to grow and being transformed that trust, understanding, and effectiveness can flourish.

It is also important to encourage less defensiveness and greater transparency to behaviors and perspectives that may be sexually exploitative, racially prejudiced, or ageist in nature. It is important for the mentor to establish an environment that both members of the partnership understand to be safe, open to critique and examination, receptive to appropriate boundaries and correctives, and exhibiting a forgiving and reconciling ethos.

A second helpful practice is for the mentor to encourage the mentee to establish relationships with persons of his or her own gender, race, or age as a way to enhance the mentoring relationship. I have often encouraged persons I have mentored to seek others to mentor them in particular ways that may not be within my own gift inventory. Although I have had formative mentoring relationships with many women entering ministry or seeking their vocation in Christ, I have not faced many of the obstacles and dynamics they experience. To be sure, we often had similar experiences we could share. However, it proved invaluable to have another woman as part of the "mentoring team" to add a different presence and experience.

It is a deeply held conviction that mentoring relationships are marked by confidentiality. Yet they are not marked by exclusivity. Many persons who have turned to me for primary mentoring have benefited richly from relationships they established with persons who share their gender, race, or age. I have welcomed such relationships. These experiences have enriched my understanding as a mentor and a partner in leadership. At times they have challenged my understanding and called me to repentance for my inherent sexism, racism, or ageism. And they have offered me renewal in my capacity to mentor across gender distinctions, racial differences, and age disparity. In so doing, they have provided a renewed experience of the inclusive community of Christ.

The third practice I recommend is for mentors to enter into mentoring relationships with the conviction that they will have mentors of their own. I have made it a habit to seek out persons of different gender, race, and age to mentor me. This has kept me acutely aware of my own

144

assumptions and the dynamics of meaning that we experience. These relationships have also engendered humility and thankfulness for the gift of difference and the precious unity we share in our calling in Christ. The great labors of these theologians of liberation, pastoral psychology colleagues, and others who travel with us in these relationships are critical companions in this important aspect of the mentoring journey.

Text—Context—Textile

While conducting a workshop on the mentoring process for ministry preparation in the Mississippi Annual Conference, I began developing the relationship between text and context. One of the members of the conference got rather excited about the way in which the context could be read by the text and how the context affected the way in which the text was read.

I had written the concept on newsprint and posted it for the gathering to see. My excited colleague asked to come forward and draw a possible "non-linear" way of understanding the concept. Multiple lines were drawn vertically and labeled "text." Horizontal lines were drawn across them and labeled "context." A rather wavy box was drawn around the whole of it and labeled "textile."

The cloth that covers us in ministry is woven from the textual warp and the contextual woof. Does it stretch the metaphor too far to wonder whose design is on the cloth or whose hand is at the shuttle? The illustrator drew back from the drawing and seemed to have the answer, "Now I know what role I play!"

Credo

"Who do people say that the Son of Man is?" (Matt. 16:13).

This is the crucial question put to Peter and the disciples by Jesus. It remains the key question in the mentoring relationship: "Who do you say that I am?"

Remember the story?

Now when Jesus came into the district of Caesarea Philippi, he asked his disciples, "Who do people say that the Son of Man is?" And they said, "Some say John the Baptist, but others Elijah, and still others Jeremiah or one of the prophets." He said to them, "But who do you say that I am?" Simon Peter answered, "You are the Messiah, the Son of the living God." And Jesus answered him, "Blessed are you, Simon son of Jonah! For flesh and blood has not revealed this to you, but my Father in heaven. And I tell you, you are Peter, and on this rock I will build my church, and the gates of Hades will not prevail against it. I will give you the keys of the kingdom of heaven, and whatever you bind on earth will be bound in heaven, and whatever you loose on earth will be loosed in heaven." (Matt. 16:13–19)

It is the pivotal moment when Peter makes a personal declaration of faith emerging out of his experience with Jesus. It is clear from his answer that Peter is immersed in the Messianic hope and teaching of the rabbis. He is also able to report the confessions and Christologies of others with clarity. It seems that Peter must have been aware of the impact of these claims about Jesus. However, it is Peter's confession and those of the other disciples that interest Jesus.

So it is with the mentoring relationship. Liturgically and academically engaged in the practices and theology of the great creeds, confessions, and doctrines of the church as well as being surrounded by the experience and declarations of the great cloud of witnesses, the mentoring relationship requires the question of Jesus to be ever present. "Who do *you* say that I am?"

The importance and gravity of this exercise in confessional theology are framed by the response Jesus makes to Peter. Some may see Jesus' claiming Peter as the foundation of the church as an exclusive act. However, even those traditions that exalt Peter's confession and his role as the foundation of the church continue the tradition through ordination into his apostolic ministry. For others, Peter's example is one we are called to emulate and express in our own experience. In either case, it is important to embrace the fact that the foundation of the church falls squarely on the edifying confession and vocational direction that will follow from it. A clear witness to the Incarnation, revealed by God in our experience, is the foundation of the church.

It is incumbent upon the mentor to continue to raise Jesus' inquiry "Who do you say that I am?" as they journey together. It is part of the

146

Wesleyan tradition to ask, "Where have you seen or met Jesus this week?" as part of the ritual of *koinonia*. It is to develop within a person who is responding to the call to Christian vocation a capacity to be attuned to and respond to God's presence as a way of being—a *theological habitus.*[21]

One of the crucial concerns that ecclesiastical boards and ministry committees share with seminaries and field supervisors is the difficulty many candidates have in "theological reflection" or "expressing their Christology" or "being passionate and integrated in their theology." Theological faculties often find this bemusing, since the candidates who raised concern in ecclesiastical examination frequently were academically well prepared and clearly able to use the resources of the academy. They could report accurately what *others* have said and what that might mean. Yet, in the context of Jesus' question to Peter, they could not make a confession based on their *own* experience and confrontation with God's work in the world or the companionship of the living Christ whose presence makes our "hearts [burn] within us" (Luke 24:32).

What is needed is a clear agenda for the mentoring relationship. It is what the *Book of Discipline* lays out as "our theological task." It is the exercise of Peter and the disciples. It was the task of Priscilla in her house meetings across the growing Christian church. It was the work of those who gathered around the table with Martin Luther to talk. It was the exercise of the Methodist class meetings. It is the exercise of Solentiname and base communities like it. It is the exercise called for by John Cobb in his vision of "reclaiming the church."

> [A]lthough these liberationist theologies sometimes show how pastors and lay people can be engaged in theological reflection, they do not immediately involve the dominant oldline community in doing its own theology. This community either takes a tolerant interest in what these groups do, or it becomes defensive toward them. Neither stance has yet led to serious theological reflection.
>
> The professionalization of theologians and the transformation of theology into an academic discipline would not be so disturbing if ministers and lay Christians had found another way to reflect as Christians about the issues they face. The label *theology* is not the issue. But with the abandonment of theology by the church has gone the abandonment of intentional Christian thinking in general. This has gone so far that

church leaders can hardly envision the formation of reflection groups within the churches to consider the questions that face us. Some reflection about personal issues in light of Bible study is as far as most believe it is possible to go.[22]

In my experience of mentoring, the work of credo is foreboding at first. I get the sense that mentees are afraid they will make a mistake. Initially, the work seems impenetrable and something that someone else with more expertise, wisdom, or study than the mentee should do. Except, mentees usually have enough to begin to tell the story.

In telling the story they know—Scripture or the tradition of the church or the experience of their local community of faith or their family or themselves—mentees have begun to make claims about God for themselves. With the mentor's care and guidance, the mentee's capacity to put the riches of the scriptural story, the reflection of the tradition, and his or her own experience into a comprehensible confession grows and becomes more articulate. It is not just an articulation of the intellect but an integration of one's very being with the story and activity of God, claiming one's devotion, eliciting one's praise, and being persuasive and edifying in the testimony of one's life.

I think of the role Philip had in the faith journey of the eunuch of Ethiopia. You remember that the scroll of the prophet Isaiah was the text being read. I love the Spirit's instruction to Philip, "Go over to this chariot and join it." That is the fundamental charge and invitation of mentoring. Then there is Philip's inquiry, "Do you understand what you are reading?" And the response, "How can I, unless someone guides me?" (Acts 8:26–40). The end of the story is one of baptism and praise. That is the hope of the focus on *credo*: the capacity of the mentor to guide the mentee in reading the text and the context in light of the articulation of God's reality and of a testimony of faith and understanding. "This I believe!"

It is the foundational reality of the church and empowering testimony that vitalizes the vocation of the individual—*and* that of the church. In the opening sections of *The Book of Discipline*, The United Methodist Church has commended this process as the critical work of the whole church. The wisdom offered to the church focuses the mentoring relationship. They are instructional, inviting, challenging, and stirring words that embrace a sacred trust given to those who were given the keys and must respond to the particular inquiry, "Who do you say that I am?"

Theology is our effort to reflect upon God's gracious action in our lives. In response to the love of Christ, we desire to be drawn into a deeper relationship with the "author and perfecter of our faith." Our theological explorations seek to give expression to the mysterious reality of God's presence, peace, and power in the world. By so doing, we attempt to articulate more clearly our understanding of the divine-human encounter and are thereby more fully prepared to participate in God's work in the world.

The theological task, though related to the Church's doctrinal expressions, serves a different function. Our doctrinal affirmations assist us in the discernment of Christian truth in ever-changing contexts. Our theological task includes the testing, renewal, elaboration, and application of our doctrinal perspective in carrying out our calling "to spread scriptural holiness over these lands."

While the Church considers its doctrinal affirmations a central feature of its identity and restricts official changes to a constitutional process, the Church encourages serious reflection across the theological spectrum. . . .

[Our theological task] requires the participation of all who are in our Church, lay and ordained, because the mission of the Church is to be carried out by everyone who is called to discipleship. To be persons of faith is to hunger to understand the truth given to us in Jesus Christ.

Theological inquiry is by no means a casual undertaking. It requires sustained disciplines of study, reflection, and prayer.

Yet the discernment of "plain truth for plain people" is not limited to theological specialists. Scholars have their role to play in assisting the people of God to fulfill this calling, but all Christians are called to theological reflection. . . .

Our theological task is contextual and incarnational. It is grounded upon God's supreme mode of self-revelation—the incarnation in Jesus Christ. God's eternal Word comes to us in flesh and blood in a given time and place, and in full identification with humanity. Therefore, theological reflection is energized by our incarnational involvement in the daily life of the Church and the world, as we participate in God's liberating and saving action.

Our theological task is essentially practical. It informs the individual's daily decisions and serves the Church's life and work. While highly theoretical constructions of Christian thought make important contributions to theological understanding, we finally measure the truth of such statements in relation to their practical significance. Our interest is to incorporate the promises and demands of the gospel into our daily lives.

Theological inquiry can clarify our thinking about what we are to say and do. It presses us to pay attention to the world around us.[23]

The late Dr. Harrell Beck taught Old Testament to generations of students at Boston University School of Theology. More than the academic acuity we gained was the formation he commended for pastors and leaders in the church. The importance of knowing the ways of God in the Hebrew Bible were matters of knowing the wonderful ways of God in our contemporary context.

One day we were to have an exam. The class gathered; a hush was in the room as last-minute studying and referencing were taking place. Dr. Beck entered the room, with his customary smile that engulfed his whole face and radiated joy through a presence that combined prophet and patriarch. "You have the privilege of doing biblical theology today. Let us stand and praise God with a psalm [Psalm 150] of the sweet singer of Israel. Repeating each line after me . . ."

> Praise the LORD!
> Praise God in his sanctuary;
>   praise him in his mighty firmament!
> Praise him for his mighty deeds;
>   praise him according to his surpassing greatness!
> Praise him with trumpet sound;
>   praise him with lute and harp!
> Praise him with tambourine and dance;
>   praise him with strings and pipe!
> Praise him with clanging cymbals;
>   praise him with loud clashing cymbals!
> Let everything that breathes praise the LORD!
> Praise the LORD!

"Then let us do biblical theology as an expression of praise to God!" he exclaimed.

And so, the work of credo and theological reflection and confession are liturgical in nature and form the foundational commitment of our lives as we claim what God has done and what we have seen and believed.

Connexion

For as long as I have been attending annual conference, the opening hymn of the clergy session has been Charles Wesley's "And Are We Yet Alive." I fondly remember the eldest members of our collegium greeting one another with warm tenderness that embodied the spiritual unity of the United Methodist connexion. I have cherished the times when a period of the session was set aside for sharing among the colleagues. There have been times of witness to the fruit of the gospel in a field of ministry. There have also been difficult confrontations when a member has violated the covenant. Repentance, rehabilitation, and reconciliation were held as sacred work. I recall times when we have held one another accountable for the best ideals of the gospel and the commitment we would make as leaders of the church and in our personal discipleship.

To this day I sing the hymn with tears in my eyes. I cherish the bonds of connexion and the corporate care for the church and its clergy that have been shared among us over these years. I cherish the accountability, the suffering we have done on one another's behalf, the disappointment, the grace, the joy, and the hope. When we endeavor to mentor a person into Christian vocation, especially into clergy leadership, we must do so with the awareness of the best ideals of the connexion of which we are a part.

> And are we yet alive, and see each other's face?
> Glory and thanks to Jesus give for his almighty grace!
>
> Preserved by power divine to full salvation here,
> again in Jesus' praise we join, and in his sight appear.
>
> What troubles have we seen, what mighty conflicts past,
> fightings without, and fears within, since we assembled last!
>
> Yet out of all the Lord has brought us by his love;
> and still he doth his help afford, and hides our life above.

Then let us make our boast of his redeeming power,
which saves us to the uttermost, till we can sin no more.

Let us take up the cross till we the crown obtain,
and gladly reckon all things loss so we may Jesus gain.[24]

Collegiality and Empowering Evaluation

There is a deep sense of connexion that comes to United Methodists across the experience of the church. It is as spiritual and vocational as it is structural and organizational. It was cherished in the *koinonia* of the class meeting and the collegiality of the itinerants. Spiritual and vocational identity and growth were intimately related to accountability, with its responsibility for correction and confession as well as with blessing and assurance of grace.

The clergy in my annual conference were brought together in regional clusters. We met with the district superintendent once a month. My first introduction to the cluster meeting was as a student local pastor while in seminary. That setting fostered in me the feeling of connexion and mutual ministry. The sense that my ministry was part of the larger work of the church was incarnate in the sharing done around the table. We held one another accountable for the work we were doing, sharing intimately the struggles and joys in our individual appointments. However, our covenant of ministry in the annual conference empowered us to companion one another in such a way that we felt a mutual responsibility to contribute to one another's ministry through strategic suggestions, encouragement, holding one another accountable for our leadership, and growth in grace and effectiveness. The district superintendent joined in these conversations as a colleague. There was sharing from the cabinet meetings about the work of the cluster and a sense of their own process and vulnerability. It was clear that evaluation was being conducted in these times together, but it was evaluation that truly "valued" our gifts and graces as well as being clear about where improvement and learning needed to take place.

The cluster grew in trust together. We were there for one another, being the incarnate promise of the presence of Christ. As happens to United Methodist clergy, there were times when a move was pending and vocational issues were before us. We openly discussed strengths and weaknesses, the vitality of call, and the direction of discipleship. The spirit of that cluster sustained me through my election to probationary membership and entry into connexional ministry.

That model of connexion and mutual support, encouragement, and evaluation continued through another appointment and midway through a third. Then it came to an end when the annual conference reorganized and the superintendents were deployed so as to use their time more "efficiently." Evaluation became a yearly, formal affair. It took a more personal and private form. It seemed evaluation had more to do with appointment making than with the consistent empowerment for ministry the regular mutual mentoring and evaluation of the cluster provided.

Connected by Grace and Vocation or the Machinery of Organization?

A perennial temptation for the Methodist movement is to leave behind its peculiar gift of mentoring *koinonia* in the class meeting and in circuits and clusters of clergy in favor of more "efficient" or organizationally more "effective" strategies of structure and bureaucracy. As the number of Methodists grew on both sides of the Atlantic at the turn of the eighteenth century, the ministry to which they applied themselves seemed to require a more complex organization. The more organic connexion that Wesley had envisioned made way for a more mechanistic approach to organization and efficiency. Discrete parts of the organic connexion were preserved in name or in part. However, the organic and spiritual connexions, expressed in the image of the body of Christ, were emphatically *not* the ones offered in the mid-nineteenth century to describe Methodism. Now the Methodist connexion was depicted as a great machine, akin to the one envisioned by Ezekiel. As you read the quotation below describing Methodism as machine, keep in mind that it was written prior to the proliferation of the kind of bureaucracy that marks our contemporary culture.

> The great iron wheel in the system is itinerancy, and truly it grinds some of us most tremendously; the brazen wheel, attached and kept in motion by the former, is the local ministry; the silver wheel, the class leaders; the

golden wheel, the doctrine and discipline of the church, in full and successful operation. Now, sir, it is evident that the entire movement depends upon keeping the great iron wheel of itinerancy constantly and rapidly rolling round. But, to be more specific, and to make an application of this figure to American Methodism, let us carefully note the admirable and astounding movements of this wonderful machine. You will perceive there are "wheels within wheels." First, there is the great outer wheel of episcopacy, which accomplishes its great revolution once in four years. To this there are attached twenty-eight smaller wheels, styled annual conferences, moving around once a year; to these are attached one hundred wheels, designated presiding elders, moving twelve hundred other wheels, termed quarterly conferences, every three months; to these are attached four thousand wheels, styled, travelling preachers, moving round once a month, and communicating motion to thirty thousand wheels, called class leaders, moving round once a week, and who, in turn, being attached to between seven and eight hundred thousand wheels, called members, give a sufficient impulse to whirl them round every day. O, sir, what a machine is this! This is the machine of which Archimedes only dreamed; this is the machine destined, under God, to move the world, to turn it upside down.[25]

In the beginning years of the Methodist movement, on both sides of the Atlantic, the evangelical piety of personal experience of God was integrated with the social witness and missional outreach of the individual Christian, or joined together in the larger mission of the church. As the early decades of the nineteenth century unfolded, a division opened up between the elements of evangelical piety and its accompanying fellowship, on the one hand, and the business and mission of the church, on the other.

At the same time, growth in benevolent organizations related to the church demanded a great deal of organizational effort from both laity and clergy. These included societies to deal with the needs of the poor; missionary societies; societies that gave aid to children and widows; and societies that raised money to care for preachers when they were "burned out" or needed to retire. These benevolence societies began to compete with the class meeting for allegiance and participation. As early as the 1830s, Methodist newspapers and journals began decrying the influence of these organizations on the class meeting. By mid-century, the integrating spirituality and the small, intimate, ongoing, shepherding lay-led class meetings were overshadowed by the grand scales of the occasional camp meetings and great benevolence societies. By this time, as well, preachers became settled ministers in local churches and took over many of the pastoral functions of the classes. By the 1870s, the formal organizational dimension of the church was being touted by church leaders as its most important bond of unity. A fundamental shift had taken place that supplanted the basic *koinonia* of the church in the class meeting and the mutual mentoring of clergy—the very matter that made up its life.

By introducing the mentoring partnerships in the ministry preparation process, The United Methodist Church has planted the seed for renewing the spiritual core of the early Methodist movement and its vital connexion. As the world "stood on tiptoe" in the time of Paul to see what the children of God were going to do, so United Methodists are yearning for the kind of experience, community, forum, and intimacy with God and their mentoring sisters and brothers that are deep and wide within the Christian heritage. However, the church *must* tend what it has planted or it will be subsumed under the organization's need for mechanistic efficiency. The seed of mentoring cannot flourish within the toxic soil of mistrust.

As a member of the former Ministry Preparation Resource Team and in the training I currently do throughout the connexion, it is clear that concerns about structure and fulfilling the requirements of the *Discipline* take the majority of time, effort, and attention. The focus on mentoring is located within the organization of the church. In addition, questions are also raised about the measure of confidentiality afforded the mentoring partnership and the substance of the report that emerges from the relationship to the examining committees and boards. The concern is to "protect" the mentoring relationship by keeping the content "confidential" or, more to the point, "secret." The reasoning goes that if a fuller testimony of the work of God's grace in the life of a person were to go to these boards or committees, it would break the trust between the mentoring partners. On the other hand, it is also felt that the mentoring partnership is not directly responsive to the "screening" needs of the examining agency. What this indicates is a mutual mistrust between the *koinonia* of mentoring and the agencies of connexion. That dynamic is experienced time and again by those who seek to respond to their call to ministry and enter the process of the church only to report the toxic soil that surrounds such a promising seed.

I wonder what has happened to the connexion that is deep within my soul that causes my heart to join with my colleagues to sing, "And are we yet alive to see each other's face"? It was in the bond of colleagues, fostered in the early years of ministry—friends who would tell me the truth in evaluation and support—that trust was established in the connexion. It was in the mentoring of clustered and connected colleagues who would seek first the grace of God in me and stand with outstretched hands and hearts so that together we would know "what troubles we [have] seen, what mighty conflicts past. . . . fightings without and fears within since we assembled last." I knew I had a place in the vocation of Christ.

While moving through the process, I had no assurance that my orders would be affirmed. However, those mentoring colleagues had a broader view of vocation and place in the church. I was sure—because I had seen them do it before—that if I did not find my place within the ordained clergy, then they would be with me to find my place. I would not be abandoned.

In planting the vital seed of mentoring within the connexion, the official agencies of the church must pause and reflect upon what has been sown. Review all we have surveyed about the place, spiritual power, and dynamism that is encouraged to flourish and flower within the mentoring partnership. Think about what that means when we must establish a policy to keep all this "confidential" and away from the light of day and from accountability to the church and for its edification. You see, the church must have the opportunity to be accountable to the work of God as experienced in the mentoring partnership as much as the one who seeks candidacy for ministry must be accountable to the *magisterium* of the church. Think about the separation and disconnection in the dynamics between the vital work of God we expect to happen in the mentoring relationship and the screening process for entry into ministry through the church's examining agencies. They speak very little to one another for fear that they will violate one another's place in the process of the organization. And maybe they will.

Perhaps the work of mentoring belongs to the established clergy orders of the church. Perhaps it is within the rich soil of colleagues who seek to watch over one another in love, accompany one another on the journey of faithful leadership, and hold one another accountable to the covenant in which they are bound that the seed will bear rich fruit. Perhaps the orders' assumption of the work of mentoring will renew the church's baptismal theology regarding vocation and embrace this work as more than recruitment and screening for clergy membership—that this work is about the broader task of mentoring baptismal vocational discernment and decision making. Perhaps that pastoral task will reestablish a vital culture of call within the body of the church and awaken persons to servant ministry, some exhibiting the gifts for ordination as deacons and elders and others serving as local pastors and other leaders of the institutional church. Yet others may find empowerment for Christian vocation in a plethora of occupations and commitments. Perhaps it is in the context of the pastoral ministry of mentoring engaged by both the order of deacons and the order of elders that the confidence of the whole church lies.

It may be too much for this crucial work of grace to be housed within a process that by its very nature must adopt methods of efficiency, assessment, screening, judgment, and the temporal needs of the church. Mentoring as more than a screening tool may not properly belong to a body whose purpose is exclusive by nature and juridical by design. The testimony of the orders, drawn from the discerning vocational work with those who seek to respond to their call, is less bound to a specific decision of entry and more committed to a faithful response in vocation.

In the Meantime

In the meantime, as mentors work with mentees and articulate their call, it must be part of their covenant that the mentor does not simply "process" a person through and "pass him or her along" to the examining boards. The mentor must be engaged consistently in evaluation with the mentee *throughout* the relationship. He or she must articulate blessing within the experience, claiming gifts that are valued and showing how they might be utilized in ministry. The mentor must also clarify and name the possible difficulties that may lie ahead in the journey, taking the authority of guide and guardian.

Given the grace that has been poured out on this relationship, it seems that the report that emerges from the mentoring partners to the examining board or committee should be edifying and descriptive of the touchstones used in the journey. The report should be written with a pure heart, a clear conscience and expression, and a sincere faith in God. Its prose should commend to the examiners a trusting place in the ultimate discernment of the appropriate vocational expression for the gifts and graces God has called and claimed.

The boards and committees are charged with discerning the merits and appropriateness of the candidate for the particular ministries and orders over which they have stewardship. This is a difficult and oftentimes vexing responsibility, but it must be discharged with discipline, wisdom, and courage. And the decisions of the boards and committees must be responsive to both the ultimate and the penultimate questions set before them when considering the call and appropriateness of a candidate. The penultimate yet most immediate and pressing question is the decision regarding candidacy, licensing, commissioning, and ordination. The ultimate question, often overlooked in the urgency of the previous question, is the ongoing attention given to a person's vocational formation and direction.

By planting the seed of the mentoring relationship, there is a realization of the promise of Christian baptismal vocational fulfillment. If a committee or a board chooses not to affirm the direction of that fulfillment in terms of ordination, commissioning, licensing, or candidacy, then the person often feels his or her pursuit of vocation through mentoring has come to an end—*the* end. Mentoring was part of the entry process, and now it is over. I have known many who speak of it as the wilderness without a Promised Land—of being cast into the outer darkness. In the connexion, this must not be the end but rather a redirection on the journey. The kind of relationship outlined in this book still holds the promise of fulfillment and an assurance that Christ and the church companion us until the end. It is the ongoing pastoral ministry we share in the connexion and affirm in the work of the orders.

The Purpose of the Order Is the Purpose of the Connexion and the Church

As the hope for renewal inherent in the establishing of mentoring relationships is planted and nurtured to bear fruit, so is the vitality of connexion renewed in the vision of the clergy orders. They seem to be part and parcel of each other as the fertile soil and the ripening seed. As clergy and leaders of the church, we are called to tend the seed and till the soil as the focus of our work, to the end that the harvest is full in response to God's call to Christ's vocation.

An order is a covenant community within the church to mutually support, care for, and hold accountable its members for the sake of the life and mission of the church. These orders, separately or together, seek to respond to the spiritual hunger among clergy for a fulfilling sense of vocation, for support among peers during this stressful time of change in the Church, and for a deepening relationship with God.[26]

Notes

1. "Hush, Hush, Somebody's Callin' Mah Name" and "Steal Away," in *Songs of Zion*, Supplemental Worship Resources 12 (Nashville: Abingdon, 1981), 100, 134.

2. *Clergy Mentoring: A Manual for Commissioned Ministers, Local Pastors, and Clergy Mentors* (Nashville: General Board of Higher Education and Ministry, 2005), 9.

3. Ibid.

4. *The American Heritage Dictionary of the English Language.*

5. "A Covenant Prayer in the Wesleyan Tradition," in *The United Methodist Hymnal* (Nashville: The United Methodist Publishing House, 1989), 607.

6. Philip Schaff and Henry Wace, eds., "Homilies of Ephrem the Syrian," *A Select Library of the Christian Church: Nicene and Post-Nicene Fathers*, 2nd series. vol. 13, part 2 (Grand Rapids: Eerdmans, 1956), 330.

7. Ted Campbell, *John Wesley and Christian Antiquity* (Nashville: Kingswood Books, 1991), 108.

8. John Chrysostom, *St. John Chrysostom: Baptismal Instructions*, trans. Paul W. Harkins (Westminster, MD: The Newman Press, 1963), 41.

9. O. P. Fitzgerald, *The Class Meeting in Twenty Short Chapters* (Nashville: Southern Methodist Publishing House, 1880), 93*ff.*

10. "Baptismal Covenant I," *United Methodist Hymnal*, 36. I have used contemporary baptismal language to indicate the intersection of Bonhoeffer's covenantal reflection and the clear statement of the same in the baptismal liturgy.

11. Dietrich Bonhoeffer, "Cost of Discipleship," in *A Testament to Freedom: The Essential Writings of Dietrich Bonhoeffer*, ed. Geffrey B. Kelly and F. Burton Nelson (San Francisco: Harper SanFrancisco, 1990), 323, 331.

12. Dietrich Bonhoeffer, "Cost of Discipleship," in *A Testament to Freedom: The Essential Writings of Dietrich Bonhoeffer*, ed. Geffrey B. Kelly and F. Burton Nelson, 2nd ed. (San Francisco: Harper SanFrancisco, 1991), 307. Copyright © 1991 by Geffrey B. Kelly and F. Burton Nelson. Reprinted by permission of HarperCollins Publishers.

13. *Fulfilling God's Call: Guidelines for Candidacy* (Nashville: General Board of Higher Education and Ministry, The United Methodist Church, 2009), 59–67.

14. *The Book of Discipline of The United Methodist Church—2008* (Nashville: The United Methodist Publishing House, 2008), paragraph 306.

15. Ibid., paragraphs 161.F; 304.3.

16. Ibid., paragraphs 301–66.

17. *Fulfilling God's Call*, 12–19.

18. *Readiness to Effectiveness*, 30.

19. See Lucia Ann McSpadden, *Meeting God at the Boundaries: Cross-Cultural–Cross-Racial Appointments* (Nashville: General Board of Higher Education and Ministry, The United Methodist Church, 2003). The next portions of this section are drawn from McSpadden's work. This book has become foundational for the denomination for the work of ministry preparation and understanding of clergy appointments. See also her subsequent book, *Meeting God at the Boundaries: A Manual for Church Leaders* (Nashville: General Board of Higher Education and Ministry, 2006). In the resource for established ministry preparation programs in annual conferences, *From Readiness to Effectiveness*, I developed the arena of multicultural, multiracial issues based on McSpadden's text. The current section is a revised excerpt of the section in *From Readiness to Effectiveness*.

20. Ibid., 50.

21. See the work of Edward Farley, especially *Practicing Gospel: Unconventional Thoughts on the Church's Ministry* (Louisville: Westminster John Knox, 2003); *Theologia: The Fragmentation and Unity of Theological Education* (Philadelphia: Fortress, 1983); and "A Theology and Practice Outside the Clerical Paradigm," in Don S. Browning, ed., *Practical Theology: The Emerging Field in Theology, Church and World* (San Francisco: Harper and Row, 1983).

22. John B. Cobb Jr., *Reclaiming the Church: Where the Mainline Went Wrong and What to Do about It* (Louisville: Westminster John Knox, 1997), 30–31.

23. "Section 4—Our Theological Task," in *Book of Discipline—2008*, paragraph 104.

24. "And Are We Yet Alive," *The United Methodist Hymnal* (Nashville: The United Methodist Publishing House, 1989), 553.

25. Quoted in George Cookman, "The Social Sources of Denominationalism: Methodism," *Denominationalism*, ed. Russell E. Richey (Nashville: Abingdon, 1977), 163.

26. *Book of Discipline—2008*, paragraph 306.

MENTORING AS HOPE FOR RENEWAL AND PROMISE FOR TRANSFORMATION

The sacrament of baptism is one of the most joyous and unifying events of the church. Whether it is the hope of new life and the promise embodied in an infant brought by parents and family or the profound awareness of the work of the Holy Spirit as a youth or adult commits himself or herself to Christ and is baptized with the name Christian, baptism is a renewing experience in the church. The fullness of that renewal is not limited to the moment when a person is incorporated into the church and a "new life in Christ." The fullness is living into the vocation baptism promises. Now when I sing the baptismal hymn that provided the theme for the 2004 General Conference, a fragment of the text of my seminary colleague, Ruth Duck, has taken on new meaning for me.

> Weave them garments bright and sparkling; compass them with
>   love and light.
> Fill, anoint them; send your Spirit, holy dove and heart's delight.[1]

162

It reminds me of the student who had accepted the garments of identity and vocation from the hand of God while walking through a New England apple orchard. These are the garments God has made to clothe us for the journey and vest us to offer our lives in service, mission, and praise. While giving thanks for baptism, the text calls the church and its leaders to be ready to accompany these individuals in discerning the meaning of their baptismal commission and in fulfilling it in vocation. This is the challenge to The United Methodist Church inherent in the establishment of the role of mentor for ministry preparation. It is a renewing sign and reclaims the model of discipleship, vocation, and ministry in which we are sent, not alone but two-by-two or joined in *koinonia* one to another.

We are plainly reminded that the journey that emerges from baptism's inheritance seeks the depths of a person's heart and being to be engaged in faithful living, joined to the vocation and mission of Jesus Christ. The establishment of the role of a mentor for companionship on the journey is an expression of the hope of the Emmaus Road, the Damascus Road, the Road through Gaza, and the road home from Moab. It is to provide a sign of the promise of Christ, "I will be with you always, even until the end of the age."

The touchstones I have presented in this book are offered to keep the attention of the relationship on the Author of the relationship and the Giver of its life and purpose. These touchstones are not linear measures of accomplishment but are signposts that guide and lead on the journey through the wilderness and make the "meantime" comprehensible and filled with the wonder of God's purposes. The touchstones help us measure the genuineness of our lives before God and our value in the vocation of Christ. They assess the tempering of the refiner's fire in the work of the Holy Spirit with us. And they strengthen our faith and courage to respond to God's call and claim upon our lives.

The establishment of mentoring as linked to vocation growing out of baptismal promise is also a sign of the connexion and unity of the body of Christ in mission. The challenges to the church and its mission are legion, tumultuous, and chaotic. The journey has led the church away from the familiar highways and byways that marked out its path for generations.

The apostle Paul, along with the early parents of the faith, launched the great ship of the church in the unknown and untried waters of the ecumenical mission that was to spread across the world. The task of those early leaders was to fit, stock, and discipline the vessel for the challenges of carrying the gospel of Jesus Christ as a beacon of hope and direction through the sweeping currents of history. By intentionally renewing the church's sacramental and spiritual center, using the organic image of the body of Christ and appropriating the vocational nurture and discipline of the primitive church, John Wesley and the early Methodists revitalized an eighteenth-century church tamed by the prevailing winds and anchored as a moribund hulk to the shifting sands of domesticated, institutional maintenance.

As the swirling tide of the third millennium rises to command the great ship of The United Methodist Church to set out upon it, the renewal of baptism and Eucharist and the attention to vocational discernment and empowerment through mentoring, *koinonia*, and the establishment of clergy orders will refit, restock, and rediscipline it to meet the divine commission. The challenges that lie ahead for the world require a renewed commitment and responsiveness to the call to join in the divine vocation. In so doing, the purpose of life and its fulfillment in faithful service become a beacon-light of Christ, illuminating the course that leads to life for all of God's children.

My hope for the future of the church lies in the experience of spiritual vitality and the growth in vocation that I have recounted in these pages. The presence of my mentors, the relationship with mentees, and the pastoral mentoring and mutual companionship on the journey of faith have convinced me that this is the heartbeat of the church. The attention and care that the official structures of the denomination give to the variety of forms of mentoring as the ongoing pastoral work of baptism not only promise to encourage the faithful life of individuals but also to strengthen the connexion for vibrant mission and vital service.

> O how deep your holy wisdom! Unimagined, all your ways!
> To your name be glory, honor! With our lives we worship, praise!
> We your people stand before you, water-washed and Spirit-born.
> By your grace, our lives we offer. Recreate us; God, transform![2]

Notes

1. "Wash, O God, Our Sons and Daughters," in *The United Methodist Hymnal* (Nashville: The United Methodist Publishing House, 1989), 605, verse 1. © 1989 The United Methodist Publishing House (Administered by The Copyright Company c/o The Copyright Company, Nashville, TN). All rights reserved. International copyright secured. Used by permission.

2. Ibid., verse 3.

BIBLIOGRAPHY

Adams, James Luther. "The Phenomenology of Fragmentation and the Ecology of Dreams," in *The Prophethood of All Believers,* edited and with an introduction by George K. Beach. Boston: Beacon, 1986, 228–29.

Albom, Mitch. *Tuesdays with Morrie.* New York: Doubleday, 1997.

Browning, Don S. "A Theology and Practice Outside the Clerical Paradigm," *Practical Theology: The Emerging Field in Theology, Church and World.* San Francisco: Harper and Row, 1983.

Campbell, Ted. *John Wesley and Christian Antiquity.* Nashville: Kingswood Books, 1991.

Candidacy Guidebook. Nashville: General Board of Higher Education and Ministry, 2004.

Chrysostom, John. *St. John Chrysostom: Baptismal Instructions.* Trans. Paul W. Harkins. Westminster, MD: The Newman Press, 1963.

Church, Leslie F. *The Early Methodist People.* London: Epworth Press, 1948.

———. *More Early Methodist People.* London: Epworth Press, 1949.

Clergy Mentoring: A Manual for Commissioned Ministers, Local Pastors, and Clergy Mentors. Nashville: General Board of Higher Education and Ministry, 2005.

Cook, Charles William, "The Disciplined Small Group in the Local Church." Diss., Perkins School of Theology, 1982.

Cookman, George. "The Social Sources of Denominationalism: Methodism," *Denominationalism.* Edited by Russell Richey. Nashville: Abingdon Press, 1977.

Dunne, Tad. *Spiritual Mentoring: Guiding People through Spiritual Exercises to Life Decisions.* San Francisco: Harper San Francisco, 1991.

Farley, Edward. *Practicing Gospel: Unconventional Thoughts on the Church's Ministry.* Louisville: Westminster John Knox Press, 2003.

————. *Theologia: The Fragmentation and Unity of Theological Education.* Philadelphia: Fortress Press, 1983.

Fénelon, François. *Spiritual Letters.* Gardiner, ME: Christian Books Publishing House, 1892.

————. *Talking with God, Meditations on the Heart of God, the Seeking Heart, the Royal Way of the Cross.* Brewster/Orleans, MA: Paraclete Press, 1997.

Fitzgerald, O. P. *The Class Meeting in Twenty Short Chapters.* Nashville: Southern Methodist Publishing House, 1880.

Fowler, James W. *Becoming Adult, Becoming Christian.* San Francisco: Harper and Row, 1984.

Fowler, Mark. *Readiness to Effectiveness: Preparation for Professional Ministry in The United Methodist Church.* Edited by James W. Haun and Anita D. Wood. Nashville: General Board of Higher Education and Ministry, 2006.

Gibbs, Mark. "Vocation, Work and Work for Pay," *Word and World: Theology for Christian Ministry,* 4/2 (Spring 1984).

González, Justo L. *Mentors as Instruments of God's Call: Biblical Reflections.* Nashville: General Board of Higher Education and Ministry, The United Methodist Church, 2009.

————. *Los Mentores como Instrumentos del Llamado de Dios: Reflectiones Biblicas.* Nashville: General Board of Higher Education and Ministry, The United Methodist Church, 2009.

Hock, Ronald F. *The Social Context of Paul's Ministry: Tentmaking and Apostleship.* Philadelphia: Fortress Press, 1980.

Holder, H. Manuscript Diary of William Holder. Transcribed by Prof. Tom Albin.

Jackson, Thomas, ed. *The Lives of Early Methodist Preachers: Chiefly Written by Themselves.* London: Wesleyan-Methodist Bookroom, 1866.

Kelly, Geffrey B., and F. Burton Nelson, eds. *A Testament to Freedom: The Essential Writings of Dietrich Bonhoeffer.* San Francisco: HarperSanFrancisco, 1990; 2nd ed., 1991.

Kolden, Marc. "Luther on Vocation," *Word and World: Theology for Christian Ministry,* 3/4 (Fall 1983).

McSpadden, Lucia Ann. *Meeting God at the Boundaries: A Manual for Church Leaders.* Nashville: General Board of Higher Education and Ministry, The United Methodist Church, 2006.

———. *Meeting God at the Boundaries: Cross-Cultural-Cross-Racial Clergy Appointments.* Nashville: General Board of Higher Education and Ministry, The United Methodist Church, 2003.

Meeks, Wayne A. *The First Urban Christians: The Social World of the Apostle Paul.* New Haven: Yale University Press, 1983.

———. *The Origins of Christian Morality: The First Two Centuries.* New Haven: Yale University Press, 1993.

Minear, Paul S. *To Die and to Live: Christ's Resurrection and Christian Vocation.* New York: Seabury Press, 1977.

Nelson, John Oliver. *Work and Vocation: A Christian Discussion.* New York: Harper and Brothers Publishers, 1954.

Neville, Joyce. *How to Share Your Faith without Being Offensive.* New York: Seabury Press, 1979.

Schaff, Philip, and Henry Wace, eds. "Homilies of Ephrem the Syrian," *A Select Library of the Christian Church: Nicene and Post-Nicene Fathers.* Second series edition, Volume 13, Part 2. Grand Rapids: William B. Eerdmans Publishing Company, 1956.

Sherwin, Oscar. *John Wesley, Friend of the People.* New York: Twayne Publishers, Inc., 1961.

Taylor, John F. A. *The Masks of Society: An Inquiry in the Covenants of Civilization.* New York: Appleton-Century-Crofts, 1966.

Tingle, Larry O. "The Wesleyan Class Meeting: Its History and Adaptability for the Twentieth Century Church." Diss., Wesley Theological Seminary, 1984.

Tracy, David. *Analogical Imagination: Christian Theology and the Culture of Pluralism.* New York: Crossroads Publishing Company, 1981.

Vogel, Dwight. *By Water and the Spirit: A United Methodist Understanding of Baptism.* Nashville: Cokesbury, 1992.

Wakefield, Gordon S., ed. *The Westminster Dictionary of Christian Spirituality*. Philadelphia: Westminster Press, 1983.

Watson, David Lowes. *The Early Methodist Class Meeting*. Nashville: Discipleship Resources, 1985.

Wesley, John. *The Works of John Wesley*. Grand Rapids: Baker Book House, 1979.

———. *The Works of John Wesley.* Nashville: Abingdon Press, 1989.

Zaragoza, Edward C. *No Longer Servants, but Friends*. Nashville: Abingdon Press, 1999.

LaVergne, TN USA
16 July 2010
189765LV00003B/5/P